TTT PROJECT

SCHOOL OF EDUCATION
SAN JOSE STATE COLLEGE
SAN JOSE, CALIFORNIA 95114

TTT PROJECT
SCHOOL OF EDUCATION
SAN JOSE STATE COLLEGE
SAN JOSE, CALIFORNIA 95114

A HANDBOOK

FOR

THE

COMMUNITY SCHOOL

DIRECTOR

A Handbook For The

Community School Director

ROBERT L. WHITT

PENDELL
PUBLISHING
COMPANY

International Standard Book Number 0-87812-012-2

Library of Congress Catalog Card Number: 70-129145

This book is respectfully dedicated to Dr. Ernest O. Melby, a MAN who helped many of us to understand what it means to be a MAN.

CONTENTS

PREFACE

Education in America is primarily concerned with serving the individual, or at least this is our philosophical position. However, in reality this is not true. Education in our land does its best to serve the largest number with an average education within a limited period of time, at the least expense.

If education is ever going to meet the avowed goals established for our society, then there must be a change in terms of what education is, who it serves, how it serves and by what methodology it is conveyed. The traditional concept of "what education is" must be changed to "what it ought to be." It is fairly well established that we in America have often confused the "is and the oughts," not only in education but in many areas of our society, particularly those that deal with the "quality" of life.

Community Education, a concept of education that involves people, facilities, and the various structures within the community comes very close to the "ought," for Community Education allows people the opportunity to reach out and find new ways and new means of *Becoming*, another way of saying that people have dignity, worth, and really count as individuals in this protean society. If this is to become a reality, then education must change. It can best be changed by making it something very real, something very important, and something very precious. This change is best understood in the context of the following, an answer to an examination question given in the author's class at Drake University.

Outside the window of one of my grade school classrooms was a weeping willow tree. I remember spending a great deal of time staring at it; I was simply bored.

One day I drew the tree the way it looked to me—a contradiction, both free and sad. I colored it brown and black, because I like brown and black. The teacher saw the picture and laughed at it— "Trees are green and their branches grow up, not down." She held it up so the class would not make a mistake of being or doing anything different.

I stopped drawing my weeping willow tree; only happy apple trees are allowed in the classroom. And, I colored grass and flowers and teachers with the crayon marked green; even though I am color blind and have never seen the color green as anything but grey. This little story is true.

The story is also true in almost every school in the country. But, children do not live "true" lives. Their world is seeing something in a cloud that is not really there, and then living with that unreal thing for as long as they can.

I like to dream of a school where a child's little world and very, very important; dreams are not destroyed . . . . A school system based upon fulfillment of imagination. Reality is the environment we and those around us create for ourselves. So, can we not create in a school a child's reality which is, I suppose, an adult's fantasy?

The child would be taught the alphabet as a key to the missing link which will connect him to the wonderful and very real, yet not real, pictures in his unsterile reading book. Science and arithmetic could be a vast mystery which is unlocked serially for years. Art and music could become the ultimate completion of a world where a child could explore unhampered in the inevitable and endless tales in his mind. [1]

This is beautiful. It expresses the need for change in a very poignant way. This student is asking that our educational system become concerned with the individual. This cannot come about unless or until the total concept of education drastically changes. It cannot come about unless or until the educational system involves the clients in writing the prescription. At this point in our social system, this can only be done through Community Education.

---

[1] Scott Thomas, Education 155, Drake University, Fall 1969.

CHAPTER I

INTRODUCTION

Introduction

As I sit in my study and look out over the park and down the hill, I see my son's school. This view, beautiful though it may be on a snowy winter day, really doesn't tell me very much about the school. The school, modern and functional, will soon be empty. The students will soon be leaving the classes, the teachers will leave the building, the doors will be locked, and the school will be closed. This physical closure is not nearly as important as the psychological closure that takes place. Within a few minutes after arriving home, my son will complete his homework, if he has any. Then, the ever present lament of a growing boy will be heard. "There's nothing to do."

Meanwhile, down at the school the custodians are going about their task of cleaning the building, making it ready for tomorrow. But, to my son, and to all the other youngsters in this neighborhood, and all the other neighborhoods across the city, today is important. Their interest in having something worthwhile to do is being thwarted by the concept that school in some magical way, as if written by the gods, is to be open and usable only between the hours of 8:30 a. m. to 3:30 p. m.

This closed school is not an isolated one. All across America, in community after community, the same process goes on. The bell rings, the children leave, and millions of dollars worth of physical facilities are tightly locked, and

3

education becomes isolated from the real life of the community. This is a particular tragedy in the slums of America, where parents cannot or will not take their children to the Y.M.C.A., to the Scouting Program, or to other agencies that offer free time programs.

Hidden in the slums of America are half the children of this land. The "Children Without" suffer the deprivations that come from lack of stimuli that are so readily available to the more affluent. My son does not suffer from the closing of the school, although his life could be much more enriched if it were open, but the disadvantaged child does not have his opportunity.

Education for the disadvantaged must be different. It must also make a DIFFERENCE. Robert Frost, a great American poet, ends one of his most famous poems with:

I shall be telling you this with a sigh;
Ages and ages hence;
Two roads diverged into the woods, and I,
I took the one less traveled by,
And that has made all the difference.

We must find new roads for the young people in our society. Their footsteps must no longer be allowed to tread the back alleys of the slums, ... alleys of despair, deprivation, delinquency and dead-endness. New roads must be developed — broad, wide roads that will lead them out of the wilderness of ignorance.

The DIFFERENCE in the learning process must come from the development of Community Education, a program of learning that takes on a new dimension that includes the concept of the "Lighted School," a school that is physically open and then translates this physical openness into a "system-openness" that will allow education to *make* a DIFFERENCE.

One of the major issues in education is that of quality. As people in education discuss this, they show a great deal of concern over the ability of one individual or group to define this concept adequately. Perhaps the best overall definition of this nebulous abstraction has been written by Dr. Alfred Schwartz in a position paper for The Great Plains School District Organization Project. In this paper he states that in a quality education program something happens to make a difference in the educational process.

He identifies the following:

1. The individual uses his talents and abilities to the maximum potential.
2. The individual seeks to continue his educational development.

4

3. The individual is able to participate actively and positively in the world of work.
4. The individual can engage in problem solving at the abstract and concrete levels.
5. The individual is developing a positive pattern of values which sustain him as an individual and a member of society.[1]

The above are all concerned with the individual. If one reads them more closely, however, there is a definite indication that education is not only an individual concern, but it is also part of a group process and involvement that would indicate that cooperation is necessary. The individual cannot go it alone; nor can the school or the home maintain a program that will develop quality. This would support the idea for Community Education based on the Community School idea.

Schwartz then identifies ten keys to quality education that support generally accepted ideas concerning the ability of educators to measure the educational enterprise.

1. Professional staff with high qualifications are employed and given the opportunity to perform their duties.
2. *Educational programs are designed to maximize the educational attainment of all the people in the community.*

Each elementary school child is entitled to:

A high quality education.
The opportunities available in a well-planned curriculum which balances the emphasis in the academic subject fields and is developed for learning experiences from the kindergarten through the twelfth grade.

3. Programs are readily available for persons in the district who need or wish to maintain their education.

This includes:

Basic Education
High School Subjects
Adult Vocational Courses
Parent and Family Life Education

[1]Alfred Schwartz, "A Search for Quality in Education," The Great Plains School District Organization Project, Position Papers (Lincoln, Nebraska) June, 1968, pp. 34-38.

5

Civic and Public Affairs Education
Cultural and Leisure-time Activities
Health and Safety Education
Community Services

4. Specialized personnel and instructional services are available to all students.

Psychological Services
School Social Work Services
Counseling Services
School Health Services
Speech and Hearing Therapy Services
Attendance Services
Child Accounting Services
Pupil Appraisal Services
Remedial Instruction Services
Special Education Services

5. Modern instructional media are available to all teachers and provisions for their effective and efficient use are assured.

6. Experimentation, innovation, and the process of change are readily apparent.

7. Systematic and organized evaluation and research are conducted continuously and the findings are used to improve programs for people.

8. Supporting services and personnel are available to maintain an effective and efficient system.

9. Physical facilities conducive to a stimulating educational environment are available.

10. Community support and understanding are readily evident.

11. Adequate financial support to provide for the essential ingredients of quality education is made available.[2]

---

[2] Ibid., pp. 38-53.

These are keys to quality. But can it be measured? Schwartz says that it can when he writes:

> While there appears to be substantial evidence that the level of quality of a school or district is directly related to the extent to which the conditions described earlier are available, the burden of proof pertaining to the level of quality is found in performance measures.

1. Documentation shows the continuous progress of ALL students in all fundamental areas.

2. Retention rates are high. Ninety to ninety-five per cent of all young people from ages five to eighteen must be enrolled in a formal educational program.

3. A high percentage of the student population continued on with education.

4. There is a substantial reduction in the incidence of underachievement among pupils and a corresponding increase in pupil achievement.

5. The average daily attendance pattern is consistently high and over the years actually shows an improved pattern.

6. Five, ten, fifteen, and twenty-five years after leaving school, individuals show a significant increase in job earnings, job satisfaction, and rate of promotion.

7. Citizenship responsibility is evident in the increasing number of individuals who vote at all elections.

8. There is evident community support for community projects such as bond issues, urban renewal programs and cultural activities.

9. The community is relatively free of discriminatory practices, and continuous efforts are made to eliminate those areas of discrimination which still exist.

10. Adequate support exists for the community library facilities and the rate of utilization increases each year.

11. The unemployment rates are insignificant and the economic well-being of the community is high.

12. Delinquency rates and divorce rates are relatively low.[3]

[3] Ibid., p. 57.

Introduction

These measures are realistic in today's cultural milieu. They represent the best that the educational system has been able to produce. If these are taken seriously, then the present educational system as now organized cannot provide all of the quality essentials. The traditional day to day program, having four walls in a self-contained classroom and operating for a specific period of time and then closing down for a longer period of time to be renovated must be changed. The school must reach outside and embrace the total community. Education must run along a continuum that incorporates young and old, learning at all levels, recreation and leisure at its best, and a concern for the well-being of every member of society. This means that the Community School Program must become the basic educational plan for every school district in this country. At the present time, it is the only quality design that promises to give a positive answer in the search for quality in education.

PURPOSES OF THE COMMUNITY SCHOOL

There are four rather broad general purposes that can be developed as a rationale for Community Schools. These are not given in any special order, only in that each can be used to support the development of a Community School Program.

1. *Economic Value to the Community*

There is little question that education contributes to the economic well-being of our society. In fact, there is a great deal of evidence to suggest that education plays a rather prominent role in our economic development.

> Economists have long known that people are an important part of the wealth of nations. Measured by what labor contributes to output, the productive capacity of human beings is now vastly larger than all other forms of wealth taken together. What economists have not stressed is the simple truth that people invest in themselves and that these investments are very large.[4]

In this concept of investment, education plays a very large role. Schultz goes on to say: "Happily we reach firmer ground in regard to education. Investment in education has risen at a rapid rate and by itself may well account for a substantial part of the otherwise unexplained rise in earnings."[5]

Education is an investment. It does not make much sense for a school district to close down a large part of that investment early each day and leave

[4] Theodore Schultz, "The American Economic Review," March 1961, Vol. 11, No. 1
[5] Ibid.

8

the tools of production idle for nearly two-thirds of each producing weekday. A commercial enterprise, operating on the same principle, would soon be bankrupt.

2. *Social Imperative to Our Society*

By 1970, one out of two children in the fourteen largest cities in America will be classed as culturally different. They will face the problems of poverty, deprivation, and dead-endedness.

Each morning as these children enter the classrooms of our complex urban areas, one of the most significant institutions in their lives will begin to function, the school. The schools function as an institution for construction or destruction, depending upon the philosophy and purposes for which they exist. Here, in the most populous areas, with the least beauty, the treasures of the mind must be unearthed. Often the tools for digging are inadequate. The "pieces of eight" are buried deep in the recesses of poverty, ignorance, hatred and prejudice, indifference and condescension. The map left behind by the "pirates" of our complex and protean society, is difficult to read. The exact location is in question. The probability of crying "Eureka" seems remote.

> The community school is a social imperative because only this kind of school can help the white middle class to the compassion and social responsibility which will bring an end to the poverty and the alienation of the ghetto. It is a social imperative because without the education it provides, America cannot heal the divisions which now threaten her life as a free society. For us in education it is an imperative because it is the only way we can make good on the promise we have held before the American people for a century—namely, that through education mankind can become the master of its own destiny.[6]

3. *Democratic Rights to be Involved*

A Community School is an involved school. It is not only involved with the community, but encourages the community to become involved with it. The Community School views education and the community as a single entity, recognizing that a prime need in our society is for school and home to be able to communicate. The tendency in our emerging society has been for the community to remain apart from the school, discouraged by the educational

<hr>

[6] Ernest O. Melby, "The Community School: A Social Imperative," The Community School and Its Administration, Ford Press Inc., Midland, Michigan, October 1968.

Introduction

leadership as the educational establishment remains aloof from the everyday problems outside the aseptic walls of learning.

This principle recognizes that people in a democratic society have a right to have a strong voice concerning their own destinies of their children. This principle is also based on sound learning theory. The concept that people learn more when they do something, when they become involved rather than have something done to them is more than applicable. A passive society with a withdrawing educational system cannot continue to exist as a dynamic, on-going productive commonwealth.

4. *The Principle of Accountability*

There is in our land today a concern for the educational development of all children. Also, running like a riptide through some communities is the disquietude that much of what is happening in the educational process is irrelevant and inane. There is evidence to indicate that children are not reaching the level of their potential, and in many instances those being educated are being damaged by those doing the education. The problem of providing equal educational opportunities to all pupils is not an easy one to accomplish. Because it is often extremely difficult, we dismiss it as not the responsibility of the establishment, and accountability rests with the home, the environment, birth defects or a myriad of other so-called defensible reasons.

Accountability must be placed at various levels in a democratic society. To be sure, the family, the home, the community all have a bearing upon the end product. However, the school too must be accountable to the fullest measure, and it can in no way abdicate from this accountability. It is a monopoly in the true sense. It has no competition. It is organized for very specific purposes. Unless it meets these ends, and adequately or better, then it has no right to continue to exist.

> Another way of looking at community control and decentralization is that it is also an attempt not just to bring the school and the community closer together for the benefit of the parents, but also to make the teachers, principals, and other school officials accountable to the people they serve. . . . . The customer is never right. There are many layers of authority, but it is impossible to pin down just where responsibility lies.[7]

[7] Wallace Roberts, *The Battle for Urban Schools,* Saturday Review, (November 16, 1968), p. 101.

10

William Glasser, author of "Schools Without Failure" supports this statement.

> From a Community standpoint, we will never be able to do much to correct the serious problems in homes and families. Although broken homes will always have bad effects upon the children they send to school, the schools need not therefore to give up. [8]

Glasser continues:

> Regardless of the reasons for failure, any recommendations for change must fall within the existing framework of the schools. [9]

Because the schools are in such a position, they must not only work to accomplish their own avowed goals, but they also have the responsibility to overcome the deficiencies that exist within other segments of the societal structure. This means that the community can expect more from the schools than just holding classes from 8:30 a.m. until 3:30 p.m. It really means that Community Education with all the ramifications that this entails will have to be implemented.

---

[8] Glasser, William, *Schools Without Failure*, (New York: Harper and Row, Publishers, 1969), p. 5.

[9] *Idib.*, p. 7.

CHAPTER II

COMMUNITY INVOLVEMENT

COMMUNITY INVOLVEMENT

The name of the game in Community Education is INVOLVEMENT. This takes place at several levels, starting with the attendance area or community immediately surrounding the school. In the case of the elementary or neighborhood school, this is fairly definable. The junior high school is more difficult to isolate into a community, and in the case of a senior high school, it is even more nebulous.

The Community School Director, in each instance, however, must become familiar with the community, whatever it may be, and develop ways and means of keeping in touch with the people, the agencies, and the power base within a certain definable geographical area.

In an elementary school attendance area this is somewhat easier largely because of the physical size. One way to develop such a program of involvement is just to get out and visit. There is nothing that says that a Community School Director cannot become a friendly neighbor and knock on doors, introduce himself and identify himself with a particular program at the school. In one educator's experience as a principal, this was a particularly successful method. One summer, this individual was assigned as a principal to a newly built school in a newly developed subdivision in California. The only way to know the number of students that would be in the school in September, the only way to meet the parents of these pupils, was to walk through the subdivision, knock on doors and ask specific questions concerning demographic data, and at the same time take the opportunity to ask specific questions about education, the interests of the parents and the concerns they had for the educational program in their new school.

From these short meetings, often in the back yard on the patio, some lasting friendships were made. Out of these unplanned meetings, several adult programs were started in the school, the most successful being a folk-dance club held on Friday evenings. This program, taught by the principal, provided a night out for young marrieds at no expense and served a particular need. The parents, all with small youngsters, needed to get away from the children but did not have the means of financing a big night out. At the school they could use the facilities, at no expense, share in the child-care expenses in the kindergarten room and have social contacts with other people in the community. From a principal's standpoint, this developed a tremendous reservoir of good will as well as giving something of value to the new community.

Secondly, this pupil survey was of value because it had an essential ingredient that is necessary to all surveys. It had a purpose. It was not a chance situation, but planned to accomplish a certain specific task, namely that of gaining information concerning pupil attendance at the school. However, there is a great deal of evidence to suggest that just visiting is of importance also. A principal in a junior high school in California, found it quite rewarding just walking through the neighborhood and visiting families, talking to the parents about problems at school, sitting and having a cup of coffee and discussing the "time of day" if that was all that was important at the time. This type of involvement is at the grass roots of the community and is essential in getting to know how things really are. School people often perceive the educational establishment in a specific way and often quite differently from the way the people in the community view it.

James Solberg, a junior high school principal in Seaside, California, has for some time walked through the neighborhood and visited the families of the children in the school or taken part in community activities as a member of that community.

> You drop in, unannounced, at students' homes, just to chat. You help circulate a petition that results in public health services being brought into a disadvantaged neighborhood on a regular basis.
>
> You intervene in the abrupt eviction of a poor family and you get the dispossession proceedings held up until satisfactory arrangements are made to relocate the family elsewhere in town.

You work on a committee that is instrumental in developing a local legal aid service for the poor.[1]

All of the above are statements that indicate action and involvement with people and organizations within the community. This takes time and organization.

He continues:

You learn, when you visit one family, that the four children have an odor problem because they all sleep in the same bed - and one of them is a bedwetter. You arrange for additional beds to be delivered to the home.[2]

Things like this are not learned from textbooks. Administrative theory is essential in order that an administrator is familiar with what is going on in the profession and a basic requirement for continuing educational growth, but it does not provide the individual with a sense of urgency that involves that person in problems that are here and now. An odoriferous child in a classroom is not a theoretical problem. If you think it is, just ask the teacher and students in that classroom.

This principal goes on to say:

Here she was, living in a little two-room shack, with five kids and no man around.....what a marvelous opportunity it would be, I thought, to get the teachers of her children to come down and visit with her and to have her tell them that the ninth-grade boy is the head of the family at 16. And when his temper flares at school, maybe it's because he has slept on the floor and is tired and irritable and hungry, and has found out that his daddy has sent divorce papers from Viet Nam, and when that goes through they'll lose $200 of their $322 monthly income. When a kid has that kind of trouble on his mind, and when you're his teacher, you should know about it. You *have* to know about it.[3]

This kind of information is not found by reading the latest journal. Nor is it found by listening to the school-home social counselor. This individual may help, but in the end, the real problems have to be seen firsthand. School

[1] James Solberg, "Community Relations, I Want Them to Know That We Care," *School Management*, (September, 1968), P. 38.

[2] *Ibid.*, p. 38.

[3] *Ibid.*, p. 37.

17

personnel have to stop thinking in terms of here is the school and there is the community. The school staff has to go out into the community and get to know it. And the only way the school system can reach out is for the people in the school to leave the hallowed halls of academic learning and visit with the people who live in the community, who pay their salaries, and who provide them the raw material for their livelihood. This may seem rather harsh, but educational personnel must come down from their monastery-like existence and legitimize their institutions. The real world outside must have an influence on what happens inside. This cannot happen unless the environment outside becomes familiar. Essentially, what must happen is for schools to develop good human relations rather than good public relations. "Public relations" has a false ring to it. It means that something needs to be sold whether or not it has real value.

The School-Community study or survey is designed to give the Community School Director an opportunity to analyze the attendance area which he serves, as well as to get an understanding of the surrounding areas that feed into this segment of the community. The reason for such an undertaking is based on the premise that all good Community School Directors must have a knowledge of and insights into the socio-economic backgrounds of the students and adults within the community. It is also based on the premise that the school is a part of the community, that when it opens its doors to the children, it also opens its doors to the whole community, and a school that does not know its community cannot serve the people in a satisfactory manner.

Survey information is obtained by means of walking and car tours. A detailed appraisal of the population characteristics (i.e., ethnic, racial, income and age factors), housing conditions, recreational facilities, community services (police, library, etc.) churches, industries, businesses, centers of congestion, activities engaged in by children, public health condition and any unusual features, etc. can by systematically recorded, analyzed and reported.

A second source of data is from the U.S. Census materials that are available to the public. Any public library has this material and can aid in its use. Population, housing, income characteristics, educational backgrounds, etc. are available from these tracts.

Such a survey makes it possible for the Community School Director to make personal observations and to interview people living and working in the area. The author did a community survey in a district in California one time. It took a full week of spring vacation to knock on doors, to ask questions, to visit business men, to talk with the sheriff's patrolmen, and to spend time

18

with firemen in the area. This information was of inestimable value to the school, largely because most of the teachers in that school did not know anything about the community. This survey provided a basis for further study.

A community map is essential to the survey. It can be either a map obtained from the city or county, or one that is made by the person doing the survey. This map can be used to spot homes, businesses, firehouses, police stations, churches, other schools, etc. A Community School Director must have complete knowledge of the community and its resources, not only in his own mind but readily available in the form of hard data for use with school personnel, community groups, and business interests in the community. This map should be available for all who need to use it, and of such a quality that it indicates to the professional staff and others that it represents a working tool of a fellow professional.

Much information can be obtained from visiting with leaders in the community. There is some type of power structure in every community. By asking around, using the reputational technique, these people can be identified. Once identified, it is a simple matter to make appointments and to interview these people. Much information concerning the community can be secured from these community leaders.

Another way of obtaining information from people within the community is to join various organizations and work as a member of the "in" group. The writer once served as secretary-treasurer of a Merchants' Association in a California Community. Although a principal of a high school at the time, the business group accepted the leadership from the school on an equal basis. This served in two ways; the principal could inform the business men of the needs of the school and the ways in which they could help, and the business men could work with the school in helping to solve their problems. The school needed scholarships, work spaces for the Distributive Education Program, better relations with the merchants along the main street, and more concern on their part for racial problems. In turn, the merchants were concerned with shop-lifting, vandalism, litter and trash in their parking lots and poor behavior on the part of the student body. By working together, both the school and the community benefited. Without the opportunity for a continuing dialogue, this could not have happened.

There are some specified "Do's" in relation to doing a school-community study:

1. Do a study early in your first assignment. If one has been done, bring it up to date.

2. Do keep your study up to date. A good study takes a great deal of time. Don't let it get too old. It has no value if it becomes dated.

3. Do a thorough job when it is done. Take good notes, make good interviews, use all the skills at your disposal.

4. Do share your findings with others in the school. It is primarily for school personnel that this is being done. Unless it is shared, it is of little value to the total community-school concept.

5. Do make sure that your information is accurate. Never publish inaccurate information.

6. Do treat confidential information as confidential.

7. Do make your survey attractive and easy to read. This is a professional survey, taken by a professional.

8. Do thank people for their time and interest. Do not infringe on the rights of people. If you feel you are infringing on their time and personal rights, do not pursue the issue at hand. No survey is worth alienating members of the community.

9. Do use others in the survey. A wide base of operations is what Community Education is all about.

An example of a Community Survey Study is shown by the following example of an opinionnaire designed to measure the attitudes of people in a community concerning various programs in that school district. This opinionnaire was designed by two graduate students at Drake University, Des Moines, Iowa, and provides the school administrator with a technique that has a good deal of merit. [4]

Dear Colleague:

As employees of the Urbandale Community School District we are seeking your assistance in a school administration and school board approved study. This study may be of great value to the Urbandale Community Schools. This opinionnaire will be the only school-wide instrument used this year by the School District to obtain a valid opinion sampling of our community.

[4] Arthur L. Langerman and James R. Walker, Graduate Students, Drake University, Des Moines, Iowa, January 1970. (Used by permission.)

It is our belief that the evaluation of our schools is a task which must hold a high priority if taxpayers are to receive maximum value for their tax-dollars. Effective appraisal of community attitudes toward educational activities no longer is the simple task of determining the feelings of a small constituency.

To determine how teachers feel toward certain programs in our schools, you are being asked to answer a series of statements which can be of much value to the administration and school board of this community.

This survey will be used by school authorities in Urbandale to determine how teachers view certain programs. No attempt will be made to identify you as an individual or to isolate your opinions. The number at the top of the opinionnaire is for data processing purposes.

The results of this opinionnaire will be made available through news media and *Take Me Home* bulletins.

Sincerely,

TEACHER OPINIONNAIRE

This survey is designed to determine your attitudes on a number of statements regarding the Urbandale Community School System.

Years taught in Urbandale: (including the present year)

3 years or less ☐   4-6 years ☐   7 or more ☐

Total years teaching experience: (including the present year)

☐

Your sex: Male ☐   Female ☐

Your age group including this year:

20-30 years ☐   31-40 years ☐   41-50 years ☐

over 51 years ☐

Your teaching level(s):

Elementary ☐ Junior High School ☐ Senior High School ☐

Highest degree held:

BA ☐ MA ☐ ED. S ☐ DR. ☐

INSTRUCTIONS

Place a check mark (✓) in the box which corresponds to your opinion. When you finish please return the opinionnaire to the school.

	Strongly Agree	Agree	Neither Agree Nor Disagree	Disagree	Strongly Disagree	Don't Know
1. Cooperation between the city government and the school board is satisfactory.						
2. Reorganization of the Urbandale School District with one or more other school districts would reduce the tax burden in the Urbandale area.						
3. The Urbandale School District finances are efficiently managed.						

When and as additional funds are needed these should be sought from:

	Strongly Agree	Agree	Neither Agree Nor Disagree	Disagree	Strongly Disagree	Don't Know
4. Local sources.						
5. State sources.						
6. Federal sources.						

	Strongly Agree	Agree	Neither Agree Nor Disagree	Disagree	Strongly Disagree	Don't Know
7. The curriculum, program of activities, and services, are broad enough to include all of those things you wish from the School District.						
8. Present programs at Urbandale cost more than traditional programs.						
9. The Iowa Tests of Basic Skills and the Iowa Tests of Educational Development have significance to you as indicators of student achievement.						

For each of the following programs which are now in operation in the district indicate to what degree you feel it is an effective program:

Elementary Programs

	Very Effective	Moderately Effective	Neither Eff. Nor Ineff.	Moderately Ineffective	Very Ineffective	Don't Know
10. Continuous Progress Program.						
11. Team Teaching.						
12. Differentiated Staffing.						
13. Teacher Associates.						
14. Open Instructional Space.						
15. Progress Report (report card).						
16. Multi-age Grouping.						

Community Involvement

	Very Effective	Moderately Effective	Neither Eff. Nor Ineff.	Moderately Ineffective	Very Ineffective	Don't Know
Junior High School						
17. Modular Scheduling.						
18. Large and Small Group Instruction.						
19. Teacher Associates.						
20. Independent Study.						
21. Team Teaching.						
22. Open Instructional Space (7th grade).						

High School						
23. Campus Plan and Free-Time Options.						
24. Non-Graded Curriculum.						
25. Elective Courses.						
26. Flexible Scheduling.						
27. Extensive use of Resource People and the Community Resources in the Educational Program.						
28. Independent Study Plan.						
29. Large and Small Group Instruction and/or Team Teaching.						

In general, the programs on the preceding page in Urbandale schools are more satisfactory than traditional programs of a few years ago in terms of:

	Strongly Agree	Agree	Neither Agree Nor Disagree	Disagree	Strongly Disagree	Don't Know
30. Students in Urbandale are happier in present day programs than in those of a few years ago.						
31. Current programs in Urbandale are helping students to think more creatively than in programs of a few years ago.						
32. Present programs in Urbandale help students become more responsible for their behavior than those programs of the past.						

33. Teachers are supplied with enough instructional materials to satisfactorily perform their teaching duties in Urbandale's program.						
34. Elementary school library facilities are satisfactory.						
35. Junior high school library facilities are satisfactory.						
36 High school library facilities are satisfactory.						
37. The members of the teaching staff perform their teaching duties satisfactorily.						
38. You understand the philosophy and objectives of the Urbandale School District.						

Community Involvement

	Strongly Agree	Agree	Neither Agree Nor Disagree	Disagree	Strongly Disagree	Don't Know
39. The building principals perform their administrative duties satisfactorily.						
40. The central office staff (Superintendent, Asst. Superintendent, Curriculum Director) perform their duties satisfactorily.						

In terms of the following groups, indicate the adequacy of staffing which exists in the district:	Markedly Overstaffed	Moderately Overstaffed	Adequately Staffed	Moderately Understaffed	Markedly Understaffed	No Opinion
41. Elementary teachers.						
42. Junior high teachers.						
43. Senior high teachers.						
44. Specialists (librarians, counselors, and nurses).						
45. Principals.						
46. Central office administrators.						

	Strongly Agree	Agree	Neither Agree Nor Disagree	Disagree	Strongly Disagree	Don't Know
47. The junior high school building is satisfactory for the programs operating in it. (70th & Douglas)						
48. The high school building is satisfactory for the programs operating in it.						
49. A proposal for bonding to construct new buildings should be supported.						

50. For each of the following elementary buildings indicate your belief concerning whether it is satisfactory (S) or unsatisfactory (U) for the programs operating therein. Use (DK) if you don't feel qualified to make this judgment.

Olmsted   S ☐   U ☐   DK ☐
Jensen   S ☐   U ☐   DK ☐
Karen Acres   S ☐   U ☐   DK ☐
Valerius   S ☐   U ☐   DK ☐
Rolling Green S ☐   U ☐   DK ☐
Blackhurst   S ☐   U ☐   DK ☐

51. What inadequacies exist in our schools? _____

_____

_____

_____

_____

52. What outstanding qualities exist? _____

_____

_____

_____

_____

Additional Comments: _____

_____

_____

_____

_____

The following Community Survey was designed to help the Perry Community School with its proposed bond election. At a time when more than 50 per cent of the bond elections in the state were failing, this community was developing a new concept of education for its citizens. The Board of Education in this district had decided, after much study with the community and consultant work with a neighboring university to establish a Community School Program and build the necessary facilities. After purchasing forty (40) acres adjacent to its high school and beginning to develop a Community School Building for its district, the need for more information was evident. Women in the various church organizations were asked to help call on people in the community and complete the survey questionnaire. This questionnaire is a good example of the type that a Community School Director could use in developing a community survey.

DRAKE UNIVERSITY
Perry Community School Research Study

January 1970

The purpose of this survey is to obtain the opinions of voters in the Perry Community School District about their schools. The respondants to the questionnaire are to be given no clues as to desired answers. In many cases the answers may be "don't know" or no answer.

Remain detached and unresponsive to any answer given to you. It is quite imperative that the voters response not be influenced in any way be the interviewer. If the person being interviewed asks about questions so as to seek additional information about pending projects, your response should be that you do not know.

The procedure for selecting the places at which to conduct the interviews will be as follows:

a. By some means that is a chance selection pick one of the first five houses at the beginning of your area.
b. Begin with this house following the directions given for administering the interview.
c. After completing the interview continue, proceed to the fifth house from the one just completed. (Skip four houses).
d. Administer the interview and repeat the procedure selecting the fifth house each time.

If no one is home put the address in pencil on the questionnaire and make only one return call. If no one is at home the second time indicate on the form that there was no one at the address given on the sheet.

Return all forms to the School Administration Office by 4:30 P.M. January 19.

Voter Opinionnaire

DIRECTIONS: READ THE QUESTION TO THE PERSON BEING INTERVIEWED. RECORD THEIR RESPONSE. *DO NOT* INDICATE ANY DESIRED RESPONSE. IF THEY DO NOT WANT TO ANSWER, LEAVE BLANK.

This questionnaire is being answered by a Female:_____; Male_____
a couple_____.

This residence is in Perry_____; is a rural residence_____.

****

1. What is your occupation: _____
   If married, what is your spouse's occupation? _____

29

2. Where are you employed? (In Perry, Des Moines, etc.)
_____

   If not in Perry, what factors influenced you to live in Perry?
_____

3. Do you have children in school? Yes ___; No ___. (If yes) What are their ages? _____

4. Did the head of the household complete high school? Yes _;
   No __   : Continue his education beyond high school? Yes _
   No __   . How much beyond high school? _____
_____

5. Is the head of the household employed by others? _____
   Self employed? _____; Retired? _____

6. Do you own or rent your home? Own _____; Rent _____.

7. Do you own business property? Yes _____ ; No _____.

8. Do you operate a business at this property? Yes __ ; No __.

9. How many years have you been a resident of Perry Community School District? _____

10. If a school bond election were to be held now, do you think that you would vote in favor of such an issue? Yes _____ No _____ ; Don't Know _____.

11. If the bond issue included funds for an auditorium for the high school, junior high, and community use, do you think that you would vote for the issue? Yes _____ ; No _____; Don't know _____.

12. If the bond issue included funds for a swimming pool to be open to the public after school hours, do you think that you would vote for the bond issue? Yes _____; No _____; Don't know _____.

13. If the bond issue included funds for a library to be used by the citizens as well as by students, do you think that you would vote for the issue: Yes _____ ; No _____; Don't know _____.

14. Do you feel that the present facilities for Perry School children are adequate and suitable? Yes _____ ; No _____ ; Don't know _____ .

15. If not, why not? _____
_____

16. If any should be replaced, which facilities should be first?
_____

17. How well do you feel you are informed about the schools? Very well ___ , generally well ___ , somewhat well ___ , not very well _____ , poorly informed _____ .

18. From which sources do you get your information about the schools? (May have more than one response)

    Newspaper _____
    Radio _____
    Talking to friends _____
    Talking to teachers _____
    Children in school _____
    School administrators _____
    School board members _____
    National magazines _____
    Other (please specify) _____

19. From which source do you feel you get the most correct information? _____

20. Do you or your spouse now participate in any of the following activities or groups?

    PTA _____
    Booster club _____
    Home room mother _____
    Attend board meetings _____
    Lay advisory committees _____
    Spectator at sports events _____
    Spectator at music and/or drama _____

    If married, do both of you participate about equally?
    Mother more _____ , Father more _____ .

22. If not participating, are you interested in any of the following activities?
    PTA _____
    Booster club _____
    Home room mother _____
    Attend board meetings _____
    Lay advisory committee _____
    Spectator at sports events _____
    Spectator at music and/or drama ____
    Other (please specify) _____

23. Are you an active member of any of the following?
    Church _____
    Civic organizations _____
    Political party _____
    Social organizations _____
    Service organizations _____
    Other (please specify) _____

24. Do you feel that you are able to speak to school people about school affairs? Most of the time ___ ; sometimes ___ ; usually not _____ ; never _____ .

25. Do you feel that your ideas and comments are given consideration by the schools? Usually _____ ; sometimes _____ ; not very often _____ , Never _____ .

26. With whom do you most generally discuss schools outside of your home? _____

27. Are such discussions generally favorable? _____ ; unfavorable _____ to the school.

28. What topic do you most often discuss? _____

Another way of involving the public is to develop a Community Council.

In a midwest community various School Community Councils have developed a Blue Star Program, a program in which cooperating parents place blue stars in the windows of their homes. These homes are selected by the Councils and are recognized as places of haven for children going to and from school. In case of trouble, impending molestation, fears concerning the weather, or in cases of reported tornadoes when their own parents are absent children may seek shelter. This is a most worthwhile program, one in which people show concern for others by reaching out a helping hand, and it came about because people were concerned about children's welfare and were given an opportunity through the schools to develop, on their own, a unique solution to a common problem.

A group of people selected by peers provides a systematic way of solving problems within a specific area. This may be an ad hoc committee to take care of one particular problem or a continuing council involved in the total problems of a particular community or school. In any case, the Community Director takes an active part in developing such a council, sitting in on its meetings and providing leadership when needed.

1. Do use the Community Council method of involvement.
2. Do allow the members to select.
3. Do provide leadership rather than presiding.
4. Do bring problems to the Council, not solutions.
5. Do provide alternative ways to solve problems in the form of suggestions, not mandates.

A third way of involving the community is to develop an Adult Education Council. This serves a specific purpose of providing for the educational needs of adults. This council meets at regular intervals to decide on course offerings that are needed, based on a needs survey in the community. The author once worked with a committee of this type in a senior high school. The traditional courses in the Adult Education Program were not meeting the needs of the community. One course badly needed was a Home Economics course in the use of Federal surplus commodity foods. From this course came the evidence of the need for directions on food packages and cans to be written in Spanish. The Mexican mothers had been using dried milk as flour, and their tortillas were not quite up to standard. One of the high school teachers, along with one of the mothers involved, wrote simple directions in Spanish, made labels on the ditto machine, and pasted them on the cans and packages.

The Federal Government also recognizes the need for involvement of parents in its Title I Program. In Title I it is stated very clearly that there shall be a Parental Action Committee to help with the plans for the educational program of their children. This action is based on the philosophical and psychological premise that parents do have an understanding of the basic needs of their children. It is also based on the democratic principle that all citizens in a democracy have a right to say something about their own destiny

33

and the destiny of their children. A Parental Action Committee can well be within the organizational assignment of the Community School Director. It is a natural place for this committee to be located, assigned there by the principal largely because of the nature of the programs involved and the concern it places on community involvement.

Regardless of what name is given to the group that is involved, it is essential that the Community School Director involve people in the community in an ever-increasing manner.

This is supported by recommendations that suggest the schools be given back to the people, somehow indicating that the very people who should control the schools by some manner or means have lost part of what really belongs to them.

> A Blue-Ribbon panel on school decentralization last month recommended New York's Mayor John V. Lindsay that primary responsibility for the city's schools be taken out of the hands of the city-wide Board of Education and be vested in some thirty to sixty "local" boards serving neighborhood districts within the city. Reactions to the proposals were predictable. Some individuals and organizations with a stake in the status quo were instantly opposed—and others who demand reform at any price became automatic supporters. But between these two extremes many thoughtful citizens and educators began to take a searching look at the proposals in an effort to determine how effectively they might serve the purposes of improved education.[5]

The basic issue that stands out like a beacon in a storm is the status quo. Educational change is quite threatening. Support for change is further recognized as essential with this statement.

> Inner-city parents are typically, almost totally divorced from the administration of schools their children attend. Involving them more directly in responsibility for the educational process offers a potentially fruitful approach to the problems of contemporary urban education. Almost inevitably, the "education" that results will reach far beyond the classroom—into the homes and local institutions of the community.[6]

[5] James Cass, "Give Urban Schools Back to the People," *Saturday Review*, (December 17, 1968), p. 55.

[6] *Ibid.*, p. 65.

This is a pretty fair definition of community education.

The principal of a senior high school in California encouraged a group of fathers to organize an educational Improvement Council in order to provide services for their children's school. This group, largely of Japanese fathers with children in the school, provided a medium through which funds could be raised for special projects and programs within a school that served severely disadvantaged children. In one instance, the synchronized swimming club was invited to a National Swim Show in Ann Arbor, Michigan. The cost of such a trip was nearly $3,000.00. Here, in a very low socio-economic area, the opportunity for students to fly to Michigan, to visit a major university, to swim before a national audience, and to participate in an extra-curricular activity that provided enrichment activities for students from limited backgrounds, was made possible because of massive parental involvement.

The fathers, well thought of in the entire community, were able to bring many of the community resources to bear. They were able to enlist the aid of the Chief of Police, long a foe of this particular school (and for justifiable reasons), the Mayor and the City Council, merchants along the main street, and professional men within the community. These men enlisted the help of people that the school itself was unable to reach. Also, these parents had something very positive around which they could rally. It gave them status. It enables them to reach out into the community and provide leadership in such a way that they had never before been able to do. In other words, they had a cause, a real cause.

Having one success, these men broadened their interests into other areas. Most of them were landscape architects (Japanese gardeners in California). They took an interest in the landscaping of the school. Thus one interest carried over into a concern for students. Care of the school by students increased immeasurably. Vandalism decreased dramatically.

The student body's interest in a clean campus was recognized by a Kiwanis Club. This club began to sponsor a city-wide "Clean Campus Campaign." Members of the club would inspect the various high school and junior high school campuses in the community at regular, but unannounced intervals. The whole community became cognizant of what was happening and became interested in the problems of litter in and around schools. The result of this club's efforts improved the quality of cleanliness in all the schools, cut vandalism a great deal, and in the end, provided one of the most positive motivating forces for a change in behavior at this high school.

The interesting thing to note here was that this was a group of men, some without a formal education, interested in doing something for Community Education. They were encouraged by the school and allowed to move in any direction that they felt necessary. The only thing that the school provided was leadership and the opportunity to serve. This is Community Education at its best.

Community involvement may take other forms. In fact, any time the school comes in contact with problems within the community, then there should be involvement. It may be the need for a single course in physical hygiene brought about by a recurrent health problem, a series of courses such as might be needed for a retirement group, or an action program brought about by the need for better recreation for youth. Whatever or wherever a problem exists that involves human need, then the concept of community involvement is a viable alternative to the traditional system. The only way this can be done is through the Community School Concept.

Another example of how school-home involvement improved the whole educational process is found in this letter that was given to parents at a high school production of "The King and I."

This high school where the Japanese fathers had done so much, decided to emphasize drama, speech and music as well as athletics. The Drama Department, along with the Music, Speech and Art Departments, cooperated in this production. On the opening night, the following letter was in the program:

To Friends and Patrons:

A production of this type by its very nature is expensive. Over a year ago the Student Association of South High School voted to finance this show. This is a remarkable achievement for any group to undertake. This shows a great deal of responsibility. *This is responsibility at its best.*

When the Drama Department became involved in "The King and I," serious consideration was given to renting the costumes. The entire staging and costuming you see here tonight have been designed and made by the students at the school. To help with the sewing, *many parents* have spent many hours in working with the students. Everything from spangled hats to the finest make-up line on the little eyes has been the creativity of the students. This is creativity at its best.

Participation in such a program takes a great number of students, both on and off stage. It is interesting to note that four of the students in this play are first string varsity football players. Two of these have been elected the most outstanding athletes in the history of the school. The leading lady is a Bank of America Scholarship finalist — the Student Director is also one of the finalists. Other departments within the school have helped in this Production: Choral, Instrumental, Industrial Arts, Homemaking, Physical Education. Parents within the community have helped and are now helping backstage with the children.

The Fathers School Improvement Club is also working backstage to provide assistance where needed. This is participation at its very best.

Responsibility, creativity, participation, cooperation and involvement—these are needed before the public has the opportunity to see the curtain open on our "First Night." This is education at its very best—this is community education at its very finest.

This was a ghetto school, in previous years not known for its excellence. Yet, in letters to the editor of the local paper, the following was printed:

Juvenile Excellence

Editor Record: Recently I attended two productions by members of the student body of (South High School): the band concert and "The King and I." These young people are setting a standard of excellence which has far-reaching influence, and for which every citizen of this city is indebted to them.

Many studies are made of the sources of juvenile delinquency. Would it not also be enlightening to make a study of the reasons for juvenile excellence?

Signed,
Community Citizen.

Many other letters were printed, also in the same vein. These were the first favorable comments in years. The school had changed, and the reason for the

37

change was *community involvement* which brought about different expectations. This could not have happened unless someone was willing to get out in the community and work with people. In many cases it could be a Community School Director. In today's schools, with the many problems that the schools face, it makes good educational sense for someone to have this type of responsibility on a full time basis. There is no real alternative.

The Community School Concept presents us with an alternative that may make a difference. It begins suggesting that until we get out into the community and become involved with all the people, we will *only think* we know what problems exist within the community. Once the problems that confront a community are identified, the school facility and its human resources become the focal point for the solution of these problems. The schools become emersed in the problems of the people. The schools become involved with the people who are involved in *their* schools. Given an environment for growth, people will grow, communities will grow.[7]

[7] Kerensky, V. M., "What Type of Education Can Make The Difference?," Unpublished Monograph, Florida Atlantic University, Boca Raton, Florida, 1968.

CHAPTER III

**THE COMMUNITY SCHOOL DIRECTOR AND
THE COMMUNITY SCHOOL PROGRAM**

The Community School Director And
The Community School Program

It is very difficult to describe a Community School Program, except of course in broad, general terms. This is necessary because of the differences that exist, the man involved, the job required, and the setting in which the task is to be accomplished.

The key to any Community School Program is the Community School Director. This individual is the coordinator and leader for all aspects of the community education program. He leads when there is a need to develop new programs and to maintain the old; he coordinates when it is essential that he allow others to lead and to encourage others to move forward on their own. The Community School Director is a motivator, an expediter, a learning specialist, a community relations expert, a master of ceremonies, a community action agent, a VISTA volunteer, an evangelist for education, a custodian and clerk, a vice-principal, a counselor, a boys' club leader, a girl's club sponsor, a friend in the neighborhood, and a humanitarian concerned with the welfare of our society. Now, if this sounds as if it is too much, he is much more. For you see, the Community School Program is essentially one of involvement, and a person who dares to become involved, must be ready to become whatever type of individual that is necessary in order to enable people to feel secure and to grow.

41

The Community School Director and the Community School Program

The day-to-day operations of a Director are as varied as his skills, as varied as the social setting and as complex as the person involved. However, generally speaking, there are some basic elements that are apparent in every community school. This Handbook for the Community School Director does its best to develop in some detail these central aspects of the position, giving the basic essentials necessary to the operation of a community school.

THE MAN

The Community School Director will bring something unique and special to the position because each individual director as a person is unique and special. The experience that the person has, his background, his education, the number of years on the job, his dedication to the task, his concern about others—all of these make the position different.

In many instances, the directors have a physical education background. Probably the best example of this type of an individual is the kind of director hired in Flint, Michigan, where the school district has developed this program to a fine degree. There are reasons for choosing physical education men, for they bring something special to the position.

> Physical education instructors often are gregarious, possess the physical stamina necessary for the rigors of the job, are able to utilize their knowledge of team work and what might be called "the team approach" in dealing with vast numbers.[1]

This position requires an uncommon number of hours per week. It has been estimated that many directors may spend as many as 60 hours a week, 48 weeks per year, often seven days a week to develop the program. One can see from this, that to describe a specific school program, it would be necessary to know the individual in the leadership role.

In the past, the policy was to have the Director teach part time, generally in the physical education program within the school, and then work from after school until late in the evening. As the success of the program has been substantiated by its phenomenal growth and acceptance, the trend is to place the Director in a full-time relationship. This means that the individual has more time to spend in the community during his "off" hours. What this new development has really done is to lengthen the working hours of the individual directors from 60 hours a week to a longer period of time. To many, this has been acceptable, largely because of the dedication to the job and to the idea.

---

[1] Marion Stebbins, *How to Use a Community School Director*, "Nation's Schools," October, 1966.

THE JOB

The job is more than one of hours or dedication. It does have substance, a real purpose in its plans and programming. The key to the job is the involvement of the school staff and the community. This position is largely one of becoming so aware of what is happening in the community, that the citizens being served come to expect further involvement. This can best be summarized by a statement from a brochure published by The Mott Program, Flint Board of Education.

Four "I's" Assure Successful Community Participations

IN — Get the people of the community into the school, primarily by means of recreation and education;

INTERESTED — Get them interested. Explain the problems and help the community to solve them;

INVOLVED — Ask people to help. They are willing and able when given the opportunity;

INFORMED — The informed person is the responsible citizen concerned with improvement.[2]

A second key to this directorship is one of expectations. What does the school staff expect from this position? Are they threatened? Do they see the position as just another administrative position that will detract from their jobs and take money from their programs?

Unless the teaching staff sees the job as one that is really viable to their own already overloaded schedule, there is probably little chance to be successful.

Community expectations are of equal concern. Do the citizens see this as just another position that uses tax money from an overburdened tax structure? Is it just another frill? In the process of developing a program, these fears must be overcome. People out of school have a tendency not to trust those in the educational structure. They have been through the system and know that it is not infallible. In fact, they know the opposite is true. Their experience has shown them that in not all instances are the people in education truly as dedicated as they would seem to be, and that there are those within education

[2] Brochure, "The Mott Program of the Flint Board of Education," p. 9.

who do not really care about people. When a program addresses itself to involvement of people, and promises them that education can be "beautiful," then there is potential distrust because of the previous experiences. The expectations of the community need to be encouraged, but they also need to be realized. This is the nature of the job.

THE SETTING

The community is the setting. However, much of what happens within a community in regard to education will happen within a physical facility called the school. Much of the programs success will be dependent on the facility. Does the school have a community room, or a room that can be used by citizens during the day? Many schools do not. The author worked in an elementary school in California where even the stage and the cafeteria were used for classrooms. It would have been very difficult to have an afternoon meeting in the school, but there was a church down the block. We could use this, and we did. The setting of this community school was changed somewhat, but the concept of involvement was still there.

What about a gymnasium? So much of the program is in this setting, yet many schools, particularly in milder climates do not have such a facility. A director accepting a position in such an area would have to make some substantive adjustments to the program. Perhaps in the future much less of the program will involve actual physical recreation in terms of games and competition and develop new concepts of recreation in terms of wise use of leisure time and different activities that can carry over into later life.

THE PROGRAM SETTING

Community School Directors have been assigned to four levels for program development: University and Community College, Senior High School, Junior High School and Elementary School.

The Community College is a new program, now being developed in a few places. Flint Community College has had such a program for several years. Recently, the Area XI Community College in Polk County (Des Moines), Iowa, has hired a Community School Director to help develop the concent of community education.

For several years, various universities and colleges have been working on area-wide projects, giving leadership to local school districts in development and programming. These programs are unique in that they bring skilled leadership and programming knowledge to areas and regions that would otherwise not be cognizant of community education trends. In many ways this program is similar to an outreach program of the church, performing many of the functions that were once evangelistic in concept. This analogy may not be the best, but it serves the purpose in this instance.

A selected few examples of these programs are found at: Florida Atlantic University, Boca Raton, Florida, serving the southeast area of the United States; Ball State University, Muncie, Indiana with a regional center; and Purdue University in the same state. In the next few years, several more will be opened. These centers will be one of the most positive factors in the continuing development of the Community School concept largely because the background of many of these directors is in the Flint tradition. They have learned their skills at the center of community education, and the finest example is still one of the best ways to learn.

THE SENIOR HIGH SCHOOL

The program at this level is largely one of service and facility programming, although this does not prevent the school from having many facets to its program that cannot be held at the local level.

> The basic obligation of the senior high school community director is to make his facilities available to the entire community. He must not, however, attract men and women from the "feeder" schools at the lower educational level, for the neighborhood is still the keynote of his endeavor. [3]

The nature of this position within the educational hierarchy makes it mandatory that leadership be provided to the other areas within the attendance area. There is work with other community school councils. Assistance is given to the other directors with facility problems. There is staff readily available that can alleviate problems farther down the line. In reality, this position is one of diversification and leadership. It takes a great deal of time for this individual to know what is happening within the community around the school and then within the whole community that feeds into the senior school. This position is one of high responsibility and keen sensitivity and awareness.

[3] Brochure, Mott Program, "The Community School Director."

45

THE JUNIOR HIGH SCHOOL

Somewhat like the senior high school director, this individual is responsible for programs and physical facilities that cannot be served at the lower level. Also, as indicated in the Flint program:

> The junior high school community school director is assisted by his Advisory Council in learning how he can serve the community to the fullest, and how he can serve the "feeder" schools, which in this case are the elementary schools. [4]

THE ELEMENTARY SCHOOL

In early America the people moved into a community and built a church, a school and a saloon. There are those that would argue with the above order, but the church and the school were given high priority, even over the thirsty settlers. The school became a symbol of the progress of civilization and the ability of people to plan their own life styles. The school became the town meeting house. It served to draw people together in good times and in times of travail. The "little red school house" is more than just a quaint way of expressing a concept, it *is* a concept in and of itself. The elementary school in today's society conceptually continues to play the same role although the average elementary school in our present society is neither little nor red.

> The elementary school director represents the heart of the community school concept. He introduces parents to the after-school program, as their children begin school for the first time. It is his duty to inform parents, involve them, and get them into the school. He is the school director who "takes the people from where they are, discovers where they want to go, and then helps them arrive at their destination." [5]

COMMUNITY SCHOOL PROGRAMS

One of the first problems a director faces is the potential conflict with the regular day school program. There is a law of learning that says we learn better when we are involved and interested. The key to community education after-school programs is the word interest. Children and adults involve themselves when they are interested. Much of the regular program is uninteresting

---

[4] Brochure, Mott Program, "The Community School Director."

[5] Ibid.

and lacks involvement. When the after-school program is compared with the regular program, one becomes the loser in the eyes of the children, and this loss is reflected to the teaching staff.

The Community School Director is responsible for overcoming this dilemma by education of the regular school staff. The classroom teachers are still in control of the educational system within the total system. The director cannot go around the teachers, nor can he ignore them in any program or process. The only alternatives that remain are to inform, educate and cooperate, and that is just what a community school director must do in order to overcome any antipathy that will block the after-school programs. This can be done in several ways that include:

1. Do get to know the teachers, personally as well as professionally.

2. Do inform the teachers concerning the program and all of its aspects.

3. Do involve the teachers in the program planning.

4. Do get the principal to give you his support in working with the teachers.

5. Do use the teachers in the program and pay them when payment is due.

6. Do give credit to teachers that are active, involved and do a good job in the program.

7. Do listen to complaints concerning the program and make corrections when they are legitimate.

8. Do work to involve parents with the teachers.

9. Do expect to have problems with certain staff members, and this so-called failure happens to be part of the expectations of the position.

After-school programs, however, by and large have a very positive effect on the educational program. They offer the opportunity for growth. As this growth begins to contribute to the educational development of the child, there is a distinct carry-over into the regular classes. Teachers begin to recognize this and there should be a favorable acceptance of the after-school program. One important point to remember regarding the community education program in relation to the traditional is that whatever is done should be done well and with a purpose. The school is a place for learning, and skills that are taught should be taught with measurable objectives in mind. There is as much learning taking place in a negative program as in a positive one, only the degree of relevance is the difference.

In the past, special programs have had three distinct classifications:

1. Enrichment

2. Remediation

3. Recreation

ENRICHMENT ACTIVITIES

Enrichment activities may be defined as those that extend the school day and at the same time stretch the capabilities of individuals involved in such a way that an individual's full potential is more nearly reached. This is true for adults and children alike. It is similarly true for the very young and for the very old. Whether a person is a preschooler or a member of the "Golden Age" group, enrichment is applicable. Some activities that may be considered enrichment include:

1. Curricular programs that extend beyond the school day such as "Fun With Math or Fun With Reading".

2. Craft Project Classes.

3. After School Art Classes.

4. Knitting for Fun.

5. Creative Dancing.

6. Sunrise Singers (before school program).

7. Astronomy for Fun.

The above are in no way limiting either in scope or number. Such programs can be expanded in terms of number and breadth in order to meet the needs of particular schools, individual children and specific communities. The danger in enrichment is that the innovators may cease to be just that and fail to become fully creative in terms of novelty and need. The whole purpose of enrichment is to extend, extend, extend. The Community School program can do just that, both in terms of quality and quantity.

REMEDIAL ACTIVITIES

There are, in every school and community, those members who have not reached their full potential. This may have come about through neglect on the part of the individual, or the school. Whatever the cause, the blame cannot be placed and left to remain. This is a negative approach. Something positive must be done to alleviate the situation. One of the most serious problems in relation to remediation is that it is generally started too late. Too many of the remedial programs are established in junior and senior high schools whereas they in actuality should begin as soon as the need is recognized. This may mean as early as age three in some of our socioeconomic areas.

This is supported by research done by Piaget, Bloom and others.

Four years ago Benjamin Bloom of the University of Chicago, in his seminal study of human development, stability and change in human characteristics, plotted the pattern of development of human characteristics. From his study he concluded that half of all growth in human intelligence takes place between birth and age four, another 30 percent occurs between ages four and eight, and the remaining 20 percent between ages eight and seventeen. In other words, half of a child's intellectual development takes place before the school ever sees him, and 80 percent is complete by the time he finishes second grade. Similarly, other characteristics that make up the total of human potential develop very early. [6]

Community education recognizes these needs and provides the necessary impetus to involve the home, the school and various other agencies to become cognizant of the problem and select efficacious remedies.

There is a good deal of evidence to suggest that many of our young people are working far below their natural abilities. The loss of brain power is a national disaster and the concomitant loss of economic gain is a fiscal shame. The longer some of our children stay in school the worse their achievement scores become. In terms of statistical data, even their I.Q.'s decline. It is fairly evident that a system that is designed to facilitate learning and then has its output consistently below standard, is either designed incorrectly or is functioning improperly. In any case, something must be done to reconcile the system to those involved in the process. If General Motors operated in

[6] James Cass, *The Crucial Years Before Six* (Saturday Review, June 15, 1968), p. 59.

such a fashion—cars with missing parts, unable to run as designed, they would soon be out of business. The same might be said concerning the schools.

A great deal of our work with the disadvantaged in the last decade has been remedial and/or compensatory. Having been close to people who work at such education, I know how hard and discouraging it is. Even more discouraging is the fact that the number and proportion of children who need such remedial education is not being reduced from year to year, but often increases. Our present school system is a machine for producing potential dropouts who must somehow be salvaged. While the salvage operation for this year's remedial group goes on, the teachers in the system are preparing another batch for each of the years to come. This situation is intolerable. It is expensive in money and destructive of human beings.[7]

V. M. Kerensky writes in a statement concerning Community Education and remediation:

Every citizen in America is within walking distance of a child in danger. The danger that lurks over our children is a monster of social unrest with four eyes. This monster, called despair, walks the streets of our cities feeding on isolation, indifference, ignorance, and intolerance. The monster baffles the politicians, outwits the sociologists and economists, overwhelms educators and eludes the power and money machines. Only one weapon is effective against the four-eyed monster. The weapon is in the hand which reaches out "To Touch a Child." The monster of despair cannot survive when citizens watch over their community with the "eyes" that are "in," "involved," "interested," and "informed."[8]

The interesting thing to note in the above is that Community Education is perhaps the only viable way in which real involvement can take place. Too, the process of remediation is essential to correct the problems mentioned by Kerensky. Remediation may take the following forms but should not be limited to these only:

1. Curriculum remediation such as Remedial Reading.

2. Programs for development of the Self-Concept (Flint's Program: "Better Tomorrow's for Urban Child").

[7] Ernest Melby, "The Community School: A Social Imperative" Community School and Its Administration, Ford Press Inc., Midland, Michigan, October 1968.

[8] V.M. Kerensky, "Purpose of The Conference," N.C.S.E.A. Conference, Third Annual National Community School Education Association Conference, Atlanta, Ga., December 1968, p. 5.

3. Personalized Curriculum Program (Flint's Program for the Dropout).

4. Big Brothers' Program (A program designed to help children who lack a significant male model).

5. The Stepping Stone Program (A program for girls somewhat similar to the Big Brothers' Program).

6. School Health Program.

It is well to mention here that physical health is essential to good learning. The sick or poorly-nourished youngster cannot function at his best. Physical limitations or handicaps restrict learning. Optimum intellectual growth requires a healthy physical body. There is no real alternative. Remediation is often in terms of learning techniques, but it must also be concerned with the physical reconstruction of children within the school system.

The above programs cite only a few examples of compensatory programs. It is often the case that educators fail to grasp the true nature of the learning process and try to narrow the limits within which it operates. Learning possibilities are limitless. Other forms that make a difference in the developmental growth of children without may include:

1. Outdoor education.

2. Trips to the museum, planetarium, or special shows and activities.

3. Memberships in special agencies such as the Y.M.C.A. or Boy Scouts.

4. Overnight visits with middle-class families.

5. Vacations on a farm.

6. Trips with interested families who will share their opportunities with the less fortunate.

7. Hot lunch programs for nutritional development.

It would be well for any Community School Director to be concerned with finding as many and varied programs as possible for the development of the human potential of all children. In the future, the successful school will be measured in terms of the way it maximizes the potential of every individual. Human wastage will not be tolerated, largely because in our society it is now recognized that the economic loss to the total system is so damaging that all members of the society become losers. It is too bad that a value must be placed on the individual as a producing unit before he becomes worthy of remediation, but at least this is a start toward indicating that each member of society has some value.

RECREATION ACTIVITIES

To a large degree, the original concept of Community Education was in terms of recreation. The old concept, "give the boy a bat and a ball and the problems are solved", is not true. In the Biblical sense, "man does not live by bread alone", so it is true that recreation is not in and of itself sufficient to make the Community School a complete institution. But, as all reading and thinking educators know, there is no dearth of leisure time in our society. In fact, man is increasing the amount of discretionary time at about the same rate as income is increasing. There is some evidence to suggest that in the next thirty years, the average workman in this country will be working about thirty hours per week. This will mean that the free time must be used in a positive manner or there will be many severe problems concerning mental health. A person cannot lead an active life and suddenly find meaning in just sitting. It is the responsibility of the society to identify the needs of those living in that society and find ways of aiding that individual in all his pursuits, even if that means developing programs for "fun".

Recreation may be as varied as other developmental programs. A few listed below give a clue to the type that can be developed.

1. Roller skating.

2. Athletic leagues of all types.

3. Swimming, children, adult and family.

4. Picnics and outings.

5. Folk dancing and recreational dancing.

6. Hobby and interest clubs.

7. Reading clubs.

8. Discussion groups and seminars.

This list could go on and on. It really depends on the needs of the community, the age of the participants, and the expectations of the people involved. Here is where the Community School Director and the participants come into a full blown partnership. Recreation is an area where there can be a reasonable meeting of interests and a mutuality of concern. Recreation is something with which we are all familiar. It would appear that perhaps the key to a really dynamic Community Education Program would be in the development of an exceptionally strong recreational program with the widest possible participation by people both in terms of planning and selecting.

SPECIAL PROGRAMS

There is one area within the Community School Program that bears special consideration, largely because the eventual success of the community school concept depends upon how well these special problem programs are developed and adapted to the real-life needs of the residents of a given area.

Flint, Michigan has developed some exceedingly relevant programs that have social implications and ramifications that, if carried to their logical conclusion, could revolutionize the social system within a community.

Remediation, Recreation and Enrichment are innovative but rather traditional in terms of acceptance. All educators are familiar with these concepts, although not all educators become involved with them to the degree that is necessary. There is a great deal of evidence to suggest that we probably have the means and understanding to go a long way in the solution of some of the more pressing current problems within present knowledge and socio-psychological techniques.

One such special program is the Mott Vocational Guidance Program in Flint, Michigan. It is designed to solve the problems of convicts returning from prison to an open society.

> Almost every adult understands tragedy and defeat. We are reared on the compatibility of privilege and responsibility, of crime and punishment. We attempt to live within the ethical and moral codes of our society.

> But there is a world beyond that which we know—the world behind prison bars, where tragedy and defeat are daily fare, where privilege and responsibility are still being learned, where crime and punishment—and hope—are the perch of which each flight of conversation returns.[9]

[9] Brochure, Mott Vocational Guidance Program, Flint Board of Education.

The Community School Director and the Community School Program

The problem of rehabilitation of a convict is one that faces almost every American community of any size. We have long preached that a man by going to prison pays his debt to society. However, our actions show that we do not really believe a stay in a penitentiary is enough of a payment, and so members of society, business firms, factory owners and managers continue to exact regular payments from the individual that has served time.

The Community School Program in Flint has developed a program that includes counseling, guidance, education, testing, placement and follow-up for these individuals. This program was based on the following:

> Community responsibility is the key to the entire problem of crime and the offender. The community must re-educate itself in its method of dealing with criminals; it must cease to shift the blame to other people and agencies . . . . .

> Very few prisoners spend their lives in prison; they return to the community. [10]

A second program in this category could be classified as a School Health and Safety Program. No health program in this country compares to the one in Flint. However, the problem of health is not regionally located. It is of national concern and germaine to the educational issues in our society. How can a child who is undernourished and in ill health learn? Where does his psychic energy come from when the body has no physical vigor? How can he make progress in learning when he has physical limitations? What happens to a youngster with correctable physical defects when the family has no money?

All of these are real questions that need answering. There are millions of children in this country with defects that need immediate attention. If they do not receive them, then they are less productive as adults. In and of itself this is a tragedy, but the damage done to the human spirit is incalculable. It is exceedingly evident that the value we place on the quality of the inner man in a democracy is in proportion to the care we give that individual when he is in need of special help. We say something about people when we ignore them, when we neglect them. In essence, we equate scrap heaps, garbage, refuse and men. This cannot be acceptable in a democracy, or that democracy will soon cease to be one.

[10] Ibid.

Health services need to be designed into the educational program in order to "detect conditions among children which would prevent them from participating effectively in their academic achievement." [11]

A Community School Program would take a look at the following activities:

Well Baby Clinics
Preschool Physical Examinations
Special Nutritional Programs
Health Guarded Programs
Safety Programs
Special Clinics such as Measles and Polio
Teen Age V.D. Informational Clinics
Health Counseling Programs

A third program that is unique is the Police-School Liaison Program developed by the Mott Program of the Flint Board of Education. This program is concerned not with punishment but with prevention.

> Juvenile delinquency is a social ill, and like other illnesses it can be minimized by early treatment. This is the theory of the Police-School Liaison Program established in Flint's eight junior high schools. It has been found that juvenile crime can be reduced by as much as 20 per cent by early detection, a fact that makes it imperative that the pre-delinquent child be reached before he develops an attitude vulnerable to delinquency. Because all children attend school, this is the most logical place to reach them with preventive measures. The school and the police, as the two most important agencies to combat delinquency, are united in their efforts by means of a Regional Counseling Team. [12]

This program is valuable, not so much in terms of delinquency control but because it is positively oriented toward prevention. This in itself is remarkable because we say something in our beliefs about people when we want to help them before the fact rather than afterwards. It places the emphasis on the individual and his worth rather than on punishment. A person has dignity in this type of an orientation; we build rather than tear down.

[11] Brochure, "The School Health and Safety Program," Flint Board of Education.

[12] Brochure, "The Police-School Liaison Program," Flint Board of Education.

In this program the juvenile officer works out of a junior high school. This makes a great deal of sense, for it is recognized that many of the emotional problems of youth begin at this transition period. Early each morning the officer patrols the community, in an unmarked car, keeping in touch with what is going on in each neighborhood that he serves.

The young people know and recognize him. He checks with merchants and becomes familiar with them and their problems. Juvenile headquarters will send him information to check out each day. It may be that suspicious adults have been noticed. There may be speeders in the neighborhood. Merchants may have complained about vandalism. These complaints are checked in a routine manner, and then the officer goes to his office in the school.

Here he may work with the principal, the vice-principal, check on complaints, work on a counseling team, or just be around to be part of the school program. Essential to the development of a good program of this nature is for the person involved to get to know those with whom he is working.

The three programs discussed are only a sample of the type of Special Programs that might be developed. They are, in and of themselves, unique. They do not however, come out of a single school. They come out of the Community School Program as a whole. It would be difficult for one school with a limited out-reach to develop such programs, but once the Community School approach is recognized and accepted, people themselves begin to reach out and ask for beneficial programs. The Community School in essence becomes an extension of each household in the community, and the programs developed are at the request of the people involved. Instead of expecting the school hierarchy to initiate and administer, the initiation is reversed. The need, having been there all along, is now recognized by the needy, and the recipient becomes the initiator. This is what the "hip generation" would term "beautiful," for democracy was planned to operate in this manner. And the nice thing about all of this is that it improves with time, for the people learn through the process and become more aware of the real needs, and it has been shown that as time goes on, there comes into the program a real concern for others. When this happens, then breakfast programs, school laundry rooms for slum parents, and basic learning activities for the illiterate are not looked upon as programs for failures, but man at his best helping his fellow man be his best.

THE COMMUNITY CALENDAR

As you walk into a community school, there should be, in a most prominent place, a large school calendar, showing the activities for the week. This may be a simple and an obvious concept, but unless this is available, the average student in the school or community member will probably not be aware of all that is going on in the school. Also, this acts as a reminder to the director of what is happening each day. At the same time, it indicates at a glance the breadth or sparsity of program for any given week. There will be peak periods, and concomitantly low periods. The ideal is to have a balanced program over any given length of time. A quick glance at the master calendar will show this. Also, records of previous calendars will enable the director to plan.

The calendar should be constructed of wood; a large piece of three-quarter inch plywood is adequate. A four by eight, or even better, a four by twelve foot calendar is preferable. This calendar should be divided into seven days, with slots in the wood to allow the placement of various announcements concerning daily activities. There are some Do's and Don'ts connected with this:

1. Do place in a prominent place. Don't hide the program from the public.

2. Do make it attractive. A sloppy calendar indicates you really don't care.

3. Do use professional-type letters. This is not a place for amateur painters to practice.

4. Do make your announcements neat and legible. If possible, use professional printing. Invest in a print set for your personal use.

5. Do keep it up to date. There is nothing worse than an out-of-date calendar.

6. Do encourage the public to place their announcements on the calendar.

7. Do make sure that programs announced on the calendar are actually active and meet as planned. Don't load your calendar with "phony" activities.

8. Do make the calendar easy to read and to understand. Good communication is easy communication.

OUTSIDE USE OF SCHOOL FACILITIES

A Community School Program will require a much-extended use of school facilities. In fact, this is the key to a successful program. The school that stays open until late at night is the one that will have the greatest impact on the educational program within the community, assuming, however, that a worthwhile program is taking place when the building is open. An open facility, well lighted but without the necessary ingredient, people, is only a sham.

The Community School Director will, by necessity, have to establish some system whereby facilities are scheduled and each group within the community has a fair share of use time. One of the most satisfactory methods is to arrange for the principal's office to be the clearing house for such applications. This is a central area and everyone can find the main office.

Design a simple form that will enable people to make their wants known quickly and efficiently. Check with the main office each day and make approvals. When there are conflicts, notify the applicant immediately. A good way to avoid disappointment in facility use is to allow for alternate times and facilities. A group may wish to use the community room for a meeting. This may not be possible, but a classroom near the community room may be available. The following Do's are evident in making such arrangements:

1. Do establish a system whereby others can use the school facilities. They belong to the people.

2. Do develop a system whereby applicants know if they have approval.

3. Do make sure that the meetings scheduled go on your calendar in the hall. Make the meeting place and time clear.

4. Do make special signs, with directions, if the meeting place is in an unusual location. This is common courtesy. In fact, this might be a good idea for all outside groups. It adds that something extra to your school and its program.

5. Do keep a record of all the activities during the year. File your requests and evaluate.

6. Do require all outside users to leave a completed form indicating attendance, program, adequacy of facilities, etc. Let outsiders

feel they are welcome and that you are concerned about them. This is also part of your evaluation.

7. Do make use of all existing facilities.

THE COMMUNITY SCHOOL DIRECTOR
AND SCHOOL-STAFF RELATIONS

The Community School Director plays a unique role in education. He is in the school, a member of the staff, yet much of his work is done at a time when staff members are not present. Much of the program he operates is more dramatic, receiving much more attention than the regular, traditional day-school program. This means that the Community School Director must give a good deal of attention to Principal, Teacher, Staff relations.

In working with the principal, it is essential that the director recognize that the principal is responsible for all school programs. Administrative theory recognizes certain principles of leadership; one of them is that final responsibility for administration of the school rests within the purview of the principal. Another staff member can be given authority for operating within a given area, but final responsibility ultimately comes to rest in the principal's office.

Recognizing this principle, the Community School Director must then develop a positive working relationship with the principal. Programs must be planned together. Lines of communication must be kept open. An understanding must be developed concerning the initiation of new programs. Procedures for use of school facilities must be adopted and approved by the principal. Responsibilities for use and care of facilities must become part of the operating procedures of the school.

1. Do develop a job description with the principal, outlining the job and its responsibilities in broad general terms.

2. Do meet with the principal on a regular basis in order to keep lines of communication open.

3. Do establish realistic goals for the school's program that are acceptable to both the director and the principal.

4. Do inform the principal of changes in program.

5. Do inform the principal about new programs in the developmental stage and new programs in operation.

59

6. Do invite the principal to all meetings. He may not go, but he is invited.

7. Do introduce the principal when he is in attendance. He is the principal and should be given this recognition. Also, it is good public relations for the program.

8. Do thank the principal for his cooperation. If you don't think he is one-hundred per cent cooperative, a few thank you's and he may be.

9. Do include his name in news letters, bulletins, etc. It may well be that he will want to sign all materials leaving the school. This is not unreasonable.

10. Do receive this general approval, and in some instances specific approval, for working with and involving other staff members. Don't go around the principal in making decisions that relate to other members of the school staff.

Working with the teaching staff is also the responsibility of a director. Many programs will depend upon their cooperation, and in many cases, it will depend upon their direct involvement. One has to know these people. This will mean that extra time will be spent at the school in order to meet them in informal situations. Often, when the director is working, they will already have finished their day's work. It will be necessary to be at the school many additional hours, spending time in the teachers' lounge, having lunch in the lunch room, going to regular faculty meetings, taking part in the social activities that involve the staff. A Community School Director must do everything possible to become a part of the regular staff and to develop a feeling on the part of the other staff members that he is a genuine member of the teaching team.

1. Do get to know all the teachers.

2. Do join in the social activities of the staff.

3. Do go out of your way to spend time at the school when they can get to know you.

4. Do go to faculty meetings and take part.

5. Do respect these people as full members of the profession. Never discuss teachers with the students taking part in the various activities.

6. Do recognize teachers by inviting them to all the activities. Recognize them when they do participate.

7. Do thank teachers for their participation. Do this verbally and in writing. A well placed thank-you note can do wonders for the program.

8. Do include teachers in planning.

9. Do be concerned about using the teachers' classrooms. Make sure they are in good condition for the next day.

10. Do encourage them to play a professional role in the program and when possible, pay them an adequate wage.

11. Do pay each teacher the same amount for like services. Differentiation in this area will draw up battle lines.

12. Do dress as a teacher around the school, particularly when taking part in activities related to the professional staff.

13. Do join the professional organizations and take part in their activities.

The custodial staff plays a major role in the maintenance of a Community School Program. The traditional program allows the custodians to go about their work uninterrupted. In fact, there is a good deal of evidence to support the idea that custodians like it this way. Most workmen like to go about their tasks in an efficient manner, with the possibility of looking back and seeing something accomplished. It is difficult to sweep a hall, clean a room, or scrub a shower and then have a hundred people tramp over and through it, leaving their dirt behind. The work then has to be redone, and repetitive work often dulls initiative.

The Community School Director, with the principal, needs to develop a work schedule for the custodians that will cut down on this repetitive work. In schools that have heavy schedules of after-school and evening activities, a program of minor cleaning should be done right after school and the major cleaning should be done after the various activities are over in the evening. In this manner, major cleaning is done only once, helping improve custodial morale.

1. Do develop a work schedule that meets the needs of the school.

2. Do organize in such a way that major cleaning is not repetitive.

3. Do plan ahead for large jobs, such as setting up chairs, moving heavy equipment, etc. Give the custodians at least a day's notice.

4. Do involve the custodial staff in planning.

5. Do treat the custodial staff as full members of the community education team. Make them feel they are an integral part of the school-community program.

6. Do thank and give praise.

7. Do give recognition to those people involved, both in public and in private.

8. Do include them in the activities of the school. Encourage them to take part in the regular programs.

There will be other staff members with whom involvement is essential. Central office personnel of all titles and types will visit the school. The Community School Director may use these specialists as is needed. However, these people come as advisors, through the office of the principal, and requests for such help should be made through the same channels. Their recommendations come through the principal.

Cafeteria employees will be an essential part of the program, for quite often meals will be part of the various programs. Here too, the principal will be involved, quite often directly, but more often than not on an informational basis. He will know, but the Director will be the one doing the communicating. Again, planning and communication are essential. The same common sense and courtesy elements that go to making all human relationships real and personal are applicable in this situation.

CHAPTER IV

HOW TO GAIN SUPPORT FOR YOUR PROGRAMS

How To Gain Support For Your Programs

So you have an idea. So what? It isn't any good resting in the back roads of your mind. In fact, an idea is of little value until it becomes activated into a product or a program.

There are those who believe that good ideas are hard to sell. They really aren't if the individual involved will take the time to organize and work toward gaining support for implementation of a new thought.

START WITH AN IDEA

Think about it. Work it around in your mind. Sound out those with whom you work. Ask opinions of people in the school and community. Speak with the students involved if they are to be part of the program. Think some more about it. Make some adjustments to it if there is a great deal of criticism or if people are just plain lukewarm. Finally, come to a conclusion. Is it a good idea? Is it really needed? Along the way has the idea been improved by others? If so, can I really give credit to these people? If the answer to a majority of these questions is yes, then you are ready to proceed to the next step.

MAKE PLANS FOR IMPLEMENTATION

This is the area where most ideas break down. Men come along with good ideas, and then they can't be put into action. In this process, it is well to remember the following:

Who: Who is going to carry out the program? Will the director be involved or will there be others? Can it be delegated to someone else? It is rather important here to understand that whenever possible, delegation should be a part of the Community School Director's method of operation. The whole concept of Community Education is to involve others. A new program, with outside leadership, under the guidance of the director, in many instances could become a better program and meet the desired outcomes of Community Education. Participation and involvement cannot be maximized without delegation on the part of the director.

Along with the "who" of the program, the question should be asked concerning "who will oppose it?" Almost any time there is something new in a school district, there is some opposition. A person in a leadership role is cognizant of the negative as well as the positive and makes allowances in the planning for this point of view. There may be times when the opposition will be so overwhelming that the idea is not worth pursuing. However, there are times when a program is worthwhile, even to a degree that going against a great deal of opposition is essential because the director feels in principle the program is mandatory.

Where: Where is the second question that must be answered? Where will it be? What type of facilities will be needed? (1) Are facilities available or not available? (2) Can substitute facilities be found and are they adequate? (3) In many respects, these questions are the easiest to answer.

How Much: One of the first questions that a superior will ask is, "How much will it cost?" People involved in the program will ask the same question. A director needs to give a good deal of thought to developing a cost analysis with each program. It is good business sense. In many cases, estimates are rather tentative, but with time and practice a director can develop some skill in this area.

Such an analysis will not only include what it will cost the individual to participate, but what will it cost the school district. A director should be able to make estimates that include:

1. Cost for staffing.

2. Cost for physical facilities. Each district should develop a fee basis for facilities use. Whether they charge or not, they should have an idea of what programs cost.

3. Cost of heat, light, and other utilities that might be used.

4. Cost for maintenance and custodial care.

5. Cost to be carried by participants.

It may seem rather incongruous to a director to have to be concerned with costing out a program. However, in light of today's concern by the taxpayer for additional expenses for education, supportive data are necessary. It is fiscal responsibility of the highest order to be able to provide the administration of a school district with an analysis that will enable them to make judgments based on fact rather than a "guesstatement."

PRESENT YOUR IDEA

It is not much use to plan and discuss unless the idea is presented to someone who can make some critical judgments and final decisions. Many school directors are given a good deal of latitude in developing new programs, but it is well known by those who start new programs that, in the beginning at least, approval must be given.

Make a presentation to the immediate superior. In most cases this will be the principal. In most school districts, particularly those that have enlightened leadership, this may be as far as a director needs to go in seeking approval. In other districts, such requests may go all the way to the Board of Education. In any case, preparation for the presentation should be thorough with the use of reports, budget analysis, needs, support for the program, and possible problems relating to the issues at hand. In some instances, a good use of an overhead projector can be valuable. Regardless of the presentation and methods used, it must be done with quality in mind. A sloppy, half-hearted presentation sells neither the program nor the director. In many communities, the program and the director become synonymous. When a director puts a program on the line, he is often placed in the same position.

Leave room for suggestions. Often good programs with fine supporting evidence are turned down because of inflexibility, either on the part of the person making the presentation or within the program itself. Be willing to make changes and be willing to accept alternative actions. In most cases it is better to have half a loaf than none, and besides the half-loaf may become the leaven for a larger loaf at a later date.

START THE PROGRAM

Implementation is next. With approval, plan to make the program go. Give it a great deal of fanfare. Talk it up, announce it, and make sure people know exactly what the program is, when it is offered, how much it will cost, who can participate, and any other information that is necessary. Make sure the auxiliary personnel are informed, such as custodians, maintenance people, other staff members, etc.

After the program starts, have a follow-up announcement. Make sure people involved are considered in the follow-up. Ask questions, make needed changes, and keep in touch with what is going on when not directly involved.

EVALUATE THE PROGRAM

Evaluate the program in terms of the goals established. If the goals are being met, then find still better ways to improve the offering. If the goals are not being met, then find out why and make the necessary changes. Have the participants take part in the evaluation. Make sure they feel a real part of the whole process. In some instances, ask a disinterested person to come in and look over the program. Often an outsider can see good things about the program that are never noticed. In the same manner, an observer from the outside can see potential problems. If possible, ask another director to take part in evaluation. In the case of large programs, with far-reaching implications for change within the community, a team approach to evaluation may be required.

Make a report concerning the evaluation to the administrators responsible for giving approval. The administration needs to be knowledgeable about the various programs that are being implemented. It is quite embarrassing for administrative personnel to be questioned about programs and their success without having knowledge concerning the success or failure of new offerings. It is well to write a regular report to the proper authorities within the district.

Keep a record of attendance, people involved, and recommendations made by the people participating in and those involved in carrying out the program. Make certain these records are accurate and available for evidence at a later date.

START THINKING AGAIN

Finally, start thinking again. Be certain that ideas are continually being processed in a systematic manner. No matter how good one program may be, one success does not make a Community School. It takes many, and the more successful the programs are, the bigger the demand will be for additional activities. Community Education is not static. It grows and becomes a dynamic process within the social system in which it operates.

The following is an example of how one such program came to fruition in California in 1957.

The principal of a junior high school was concerned with the large number of students reporting to the school nurse each morning at about 10:30 a.m. In making tours of the building and dropping in at the health center, he could see that all the beds were full and that other students were sitting around, looking pale and wan.

As he discussed this problem with the school nurse, the principal found that these youngsters had the following symptoms: slight nausea, headache and feeling very tired. The diagnosis from the nurse was that these youngsters had a poor diet, lacked a good breakfast and the result was low blood sugar. Illness was the result.

The Problem

The problem was how to provide these youngsters with the necessary energy to get through a morning of classes without becoming ill. The afternoon session provided few of these cases because a majority of the students had a hot lunch in the cafeteria. Those that could not afford the program were given the opportunity either to work or receive a free lunch under the program established by the school district. The Dean of Boys and the Dean of Girls in the school were quite competent and had done a very fine job in locating those that needed free lunches and handled the program in a very systematic, orderly and humane manner.

How To Gain Support For Your Programs

The Idea

The nurse offered the suggestion that a good breakfast program would go a long way toward solving the problem. Since the first busses arrived at the school at 6:50 a.m., it was quite evident that many of the children had been up since before 6:00 a.m. In this low socio-economic community, there was a good deal of evidence that parents did not prepare an adequate breakfast at this early hour, and there was further evidence that many families did not have the money nor the knowledge to offer the type of diet needed.

The school could take one of two courses. It could ignore the problem, although the problem itself would not be ignored, because the students would continue to arrive at the health center with complaints of illness. The nurse could continue to function in the capacity as a sitter for students that were in all honesty ill.

The second alternative was for the school to provide a breakfast service. This would mean that the school would be taking over a traditional family service. The question at hand was whether the school should move into a void and take on another responsibility. In reality, the question was even more basic. It was: Are children important enough to make a change in the school cafeteria program? THE IDEA WAS THERE.

The next step was to MAKE PLANS FOR IMPLEMENTATION. Who: This program by necessity was to be carried out by the cafeteria staff. The school nurse would be involved along with the cafeteria manager. The principal would be responsible, but the whole program was really one of delegation of authority.

A meeting with the nurse and the cafeteria manager was the next step. What problems would be involved? Could it be done with the present staff? After going over the reasons for the program, and asking, answering and discussing, the people involved made the decision to go ahead, but on the condition that the breakfast would be simple hand-type food and there would be no money handled by the cafeteria staff. The final decision was that it would be large sweet rolls, hot chocolate; cinnamon toast, hot chocolate or doughnuts and hot chocolate. The students would purchase tickets in the office and would purchase breakfast with this script.

The school district was a well-organized and well-run district. Principals were allowed a great deal of autonomy in making decisions involving students and programs. The superintendent was notified that the program would start. He was not asked for permission, only informed. This was within "the rules

70

of the game." He wanted to be informed in case he was asked by the board of education about certain programs. He made a recommendation that the food director for the district be informed in writing so that she could keep an eye on the program in case of further expansion, need for personnel, etc. The teachers were informed. Since they would have little to do with the program, it was not necessary to involve them in the decision-making process. Before it was finally started, the school nurse met with a group of parents from the P.T.A. and discussed the reasons for the program. They agreed that it was a good idea, particularly since some of youngsters caught the first bus at 6:15 a.m. They appreciated the school's interest and offered to help. They offered to come and serve. This would help the cafeteria staff a great deal. They also agreed to participate in supervision.

Implementation

The program was ready for implementation. The students were given the information. Announcements were made every morning for a week. A bulletin was placed on every bulletin board. A large sign was placed in the cafeteria. Special breakfast tickets were placed in the main office. The secretarial staff was informed of the procedures involved. Tickets were ten cents each or six for fifty cents. Students who could not afford the breakfast were screened and given free tickets, the same tickets as other students. Those on free lunches were given free a breakfast also. A bulletin was sent home with each child. This is not the best method at this level. It would be better to have a home mailing. The P.T.A. announced it at the school and at all of the feeder schools. Principals of the elementary schools were informed about the new program and asked to make announcements to the students at the school. They also needed to be informed in case they were pressured by parents in their attendance areas. They had peculiar problems because of the centralized kitchen program and if a breakfast program were to be started in their schools, it would take a different pattern of operation.

The program was started. The first morning arrived. Everyone was ready. The secretary had provided the cafeteria manager with a pre-count. There were nearly 150 pre-sales. It was estimated that about 50 more would purchase tickets that first morning. It was also known that about 275 students were on free meals out of a school of 1300. Breakfast was cooked and ready. The busses arrived. Students went to the cafeteria. They bought their breakfasts, ate them in a warm, attractive facility and behaved in a very mature manner. Parents arrived to help, although this was never entirely successful. It was just too early for working parents with large families. However, this particular student body

71

didn't need a great deal of supervision, largely because they had been given the opportunity for a great deal of their own supervision previous to this time. The custodian had his mops and buckets ready for accidents; and there were a few. He also had an extra man for clean-up afterwards. IT WAS A SUCCESS. Over 500 students had breakfast that first morning.

Evaluation was simple. Head count was made by the number of tickets collected. The cafeteria manager had a record of food costs and related them to the money collected. A cost breakdown showed that there was a very small profit. This was used to make larger portions, since many of the students asked for seconds. The nurse watched the amount of morning illness drop. By going back and charting the numbers each hour, the graph showed a remarkable down-turn at this period. A report was made to the superintendent. The director of food services dropped by the school and made suggestions to the cafeteria manager. The cafeteria manager was quite happy with the program because she felt they were providing a real service. The principal went by the cafeteria regularly and thanked the employees for their contributions to the program. Morale improved because they felt a real pride in doing a job well and also in terms of taking part in a unique program. An announcement was made to the press.

In all this, things seemed to go remarkably well. Student participation was high. Free meal student participation was excellent. Teachers noticed a change in student attitude. The staff supported the program and some even participated.

Then the first negative comments came. The local paper wrote an editorial. In essence this is what was written:

"It has come to our attention that one of our schools has started serving breakfast to its students. Is this just another way that socialism is taking away parental responsibility? Breakfast is a parent's responsibility. The schools took over a lunch program, teaching of sex, and now are beginning to serve breakfast. Will supper be next; then a dormitory? When this happens, they will have our children. "We are sure that the school in question has good intentions, and the principal has nothing but a good social conscience. However, we believe that this is beyond the scope of education and the Board of Education should take action to stop such programs."

Needless to say, the program did not stop. But it did lose some of the support of the community and staff.

The above has been illustrative of the processes that take place in the development of a new program. It was unique at the time. In fact, it was quite revolutionary. Yet, in spite of the fact that the need for such a program is widely recognized, breakfast programs still make news.

Also, recognize that even under the best circumstances, with the most successful program, and one that is entirely defensible in terms of what is good for a community and its children, there can be criticism from sources that may well be overlooked.

At no time in the process for gaining support was any thought given to the local newspaper. It never crossed the minds of the people involved. The problem was there. Those that were involved were dedicated to a solution. The primary concern was the well-being of the students involved. They recognized the problem and understood the reasons for the problem. And yet, in the end there was criticism from a very powerful and influential source.

The best that can be said is that the Community School learns to live with criticism and turns that criticism into positive action.

The Activity Schedule

The following schedules from *The Role of the School in Community Education* by Hickey and Van Voorhees are good examples of activity schedules that might be designed by a Community School Director and participants:

SCHEDULE FOR TUESDAY FOR A *RURAL* ELEMENTARY SCHOOL
SOMEWHERE IN SOUTHWESTERN UNITED STATES

Time	Activity	Room	How Often Class Is Held
7-8 a.m.	Stay in shape program for men	Gym	Daily
8-8:30 a.m.	Spanish — gr. 4-6	108	Daily (3 groups)
10-11 a.m.	Prenatal nutrition for expectant mothers	Commun. Rm.	Wkly.
12-1 p.m.	Community businessmen's lunch	Commun. Rm.	Monthly

73

Time	Activity	Room	How Often Class Is Held
1:30-3 p.m.	Preparation of exotic Mexican foods	Commun. Rm.	Wkly.
3-4 p.m.	Science enrichment-— gr. 5&6	Rm. 208	Twice wkly.
3:30-5 p.m.	Boys' flagball— intramurals	Playground	Daily
3:30-5 p.m.	Girls' volleyball— intramurals	Gym	Daily
7-10 p.m.	Silversmithing	102	Wkly.
7-10 p.m.	Basic reading for adults	104	Wkly.
7-10 p.m.	Weaving	106	Wkly.
7-10 p.m.	Amer. hist. designed for those seeking U.S. citizenship	204	Wkly.
7-8 p.m.	Acrobatics & trampoline, ages 7-10	Gym	Wkly.
8-9 p.m.	Acrobatics & trampoline, ages 11-14	Gym	Wkly.
7-10 p.m.	Painting, watercolors & oils	108	Wkly.
7-10 p.m.	Desert ecology (most time spent in the field)	110	Wkly.
7-9 p.m.	Eng. II for adults seeking high school diploma	112	Twice wkly.
7-9 p.m.	Public speaking	114	Wkly.
7-10 p.m.	Committee for developing "Brown studies curriculum"	116	Monthly
7-10 p.m.	Leathercraft	118	Wkly.
7-10 p.m.	S.W. Indian cultures & folklore, univ. extension	120	Wkly.

Time	Activity	Room	How Often Class Is Held
7-10 p.m.	Music & dance of Old Mexico	210	Wkly.
7-10 p.m.	Calf roping (one of a series of Rodeo Cowboys Assn. sports)	208 (practical work at a local rodeo arena)	Wkly.
7-10 p.m.	Golden-agers historical society	210	Bi-wkly.
7:30-9:30	Teen-age music appreciation & dancing	Commun. Rm.	Wkly.

SCHEDULE FOR TUESDAY FOR AN *URBAN* ELEMENTARY SCHOOL
SOMEWHERE IN NORTHERN UNITED STATES

Time	Activity	Room	How Often Class Is Held
7-8 a.m.	Jogging	Playfield	Daily (Diff. groups)
7:30-8:30 a.m.	Sunrise singers — gr. 4-6	108	Twice wkly.
10-11 a.m.	Prenatal & early childhood experiences for mothers and expectant mothers	Commun. Rm.	Wkly.
10-11 a.m.	Story hour for pre-schoolers	Library	Wkly.
12-1 p.m.	Local businessmen's lunch with some of students (equal numbers of each but different each wk.)	Commun. Rm.	Wkly.
1:30-3 p.m.	Soul food and its preparation	Commun. Rm.	Wkly.
3-4 p.m.	Reading enrichment — gr. 4-6	106 & 108	Twice wkly.
3-4 p.m.	Girls' volleyball — intramurals	Gym	Daily

75

How To Gain Support For Your Programs

Time	Activity	Room	How Often Class Is Held
4-5 p.m.	Boys' basketball— intramurals	Gym	Daily
5-7 p.m.	Men's 1st & 3rd shift basketball league	Gym	Daily
7-10 p.m.	Tailoring I	102	Wkly.
7-10 p.m.	Basic reading for adults	104	Wkly.
7-10 p.m.	African history (univ. extension if desired)	Library	Wkly.
7-8:30 p.m.	Roller skating—ages 8-14	Gym	Wkly.
7-10 p.m.	Painting, watercolors & oils	110	Wkly.
7-9 p.m.	Public speaking	112	Wkly.
7-10 p.m.	Drama	114	Wkly.
7-9:30 p.m.	Teen dance	Commun. Rm.	Wkly.
7-10 p.m.	Committee for develop- ing "Black studies curriculum"	116	Monthly
7-10 p.m.	Woodworking	Shop	Wkly.
7-10 p.m.	Hunting & fishing club	202	Monthly
7-9 p.m.	Modern jazz appreciation	108	Wkly.
7-9 p.m.	Senior citizens' Bid Whist Club	118	Wkly.
7-10 p.m.	Human relations, de- signed for increased interracial under- standing & sensitivity	204	Bi-wkly.
12-2 a.m.	Men's 2nd shift basket- ball league	Gym	Twice wkly.

SCHEDULE FOR TUESDAY FOR A *SUBURBAN* ELEMENTARY SCHOOL
SOMEWHERE ON THE PACIFIC COAST

Time	Activity	Room	How Often Class Is Held
7-8 a.m.	Jogging, men & women	Playfield	Daily (diff. groups)
8-8:30 a.m.	Introduction to the world of ideas—gr. 6	108	Wkly.
10-11 a.m.	Child growth & development—practical aspects for mothers	Commun. Rm.	Wkly.
12-1 p.m.	Students lunch with community service workers—milkmen, T.V. repairmen, diaper-service men, etc. (equal numbers of each)	Commun. Rm.	Bi-wkly. (diff. groups)
1:30-3 p.m.	Gourmet food, its preparation	Commun. Rm.	Wkly.
3-4 p.m.	Math enrichment—gr. 4-6	208 & 210	Wkly.
3-4 p.m.	Girls' volleyball—intramurals	Gym	Daily
4-5 p.m.	Boys' basketball—intramurals	Gym	Daily
7-10 p.m.	Knitting, crocheting & tatting	102	Wkly.
7-10 p.m.	Men's evening recreation program	Gym	Wkly.
7-9 p.m.	Stocks, bonds & investments	104	Wkly.
7-10 p.m.	Great books study	106	Wkly.
7-10 p.m.	Painting, watercolors & oils	108	Wkly.
7-9 p.m.	Public speaking	112	Wkly.
7-10 p.m.	Drama	114	Wkly.
7-9:30 p.m.	Teen club—dancing	Commun. Rm.	Wkly.

Time	Activity	Room	How Often Class Is Held
7-10 p.m.	Committee for developing better attitudes in human relations as found in typical suburban areas	116	Monthly
7-10 p.m.	"Do it yourself" home projects	110	Wkly.
7-10 p.m.	Local unit—League of Women Voters	118	Monthly
7-10 p.m.	Minority peoples—univ. extension	120	Wkly.
7-10 p.m.	Sailing club	202	Bi-wkly.
7-10 p.m.	Appreciation of classical music	204	Wkly.
7-9 p.m.	Bridge club	210	Wkly.
7-10 p.m.	Committee for gaining the cultural benefits of integrated housing	206	Wkly.
7-9 p.m.	Home beautification & landscaping	208	Bi-wkly. [1]

[1] Howard W. Hickey and Curtis Van Voorhees and Associates, *The Role of the School in Community Education* (Pendell Publishing Company, Midland, Michigan, 1969) pp. 110-115.

CHAPTER V

THE COMMUNITY SCHOOL DIRECTOR,
TEACHER ATTITUDE AND THE DEPRIVED CHILD

The Community School Director, Teacher Attitude and The Deprived Child

INTRODUCTION

In the next decade, the Community School Program is going to become a fairly common phenomenon in our country. It is increasingly apparent that something must really begin to happen in education. As the cost of education escalates, there is going to be a demand from the taxpayers that an accountability be placed on those responsible for making educational policy. When this happens, the schools will recognize a need for shared decision making. It will probably come about, not because educators recognize the need for it on a rational basis, but because they are forced to do it to save their own "hides".

Because this will be a new type of education, there will be new roles to play. New roles are essentially new ways of meeting new ideas. Melby suggests that:

The moment we set out to educate the entire community we are in a new ball game. We now can no longer be separated into two groups, teachers and pupils, we will in a real sense all be teachers and all students. Some will teach as a life work, others will teach merely to learn (teaching being the best way to learn), or at least

81

learn in the process of teaching. The administrative problems now become more complex, with the result that the old separation of planning and performance concepts break down . . . . Whereas in the past we have too often asked who is right, we must now ask what is right. We need to learn how to listen, how to understand.[1]

This new kind of education will require all of us to look at teacher attitudes. A Community School Director, in every respect, is a teacher. His own attitudes are of paramount importance. An understanding of his own and others' attitudes are essential in the development of the necessary skills required to develop a program within a community.

It is also mandatory that the attitudes of the adult professional staff be recognized in relation to the deprived child.

Teacher Attitudes

A child who does not like himself cannot learn. Teachers who are over-burdened with large numbers of disadvantaged youth find it hard to teach. Teaching, by its very nature, is a highly artistic activity. When an artistic activity comes in conflict with the culturally deprived student who hates his own self-image, the classroom becomes a battleground. The "War on Poverty" is also a war on "Learning Poverty" that pervades so many of our urban classrooms.

In 1950, approximately one child out of ten in the fourteen largest cities was "culturally deprived." By 1960 this figure had risen to one in three. By 1970, it will have risen to one in two.[2]

It is of further interest to note that "most of these children will be Negroes, unless something drastically changes the housing situation which exists in urban centers."[3] Deprivation is of real concern, involving school districts, school administrators, students and teachers. "Most teachers who work with the underprivileged children today find this is a most unattractive, unrewarding task." [4]

---

[1] Ernest O. Melby, "Decentralization and Community Control: Threat or Challenge?" The Community School and Its Administration, November 1969.

[2] F. Riessman, *The Culturally Deprived Child* (New York: Harper & Brothers, Inc., 1962), p. 1.

[3] William C. Kvaraceus, et al., *Negro Self-Concept* (New York: McGraw-Hill Inc., 1965), p. 18.

[4] Riessman, *op. cit.*, p. 1.

The findings of Kvaraceus,[5] Ausubel,[6] Clark,[7] indicate that the motivational differences between children of middle class parents and those of children from lower classes are quite different and this is apparent in contacts with the children of the inner-city. The children of the inner-city seem to be more "present" oriented than "future" oriented. In addition, there seems to be a lack of significant motivational models for these children.

The roots of this problem of cultural deprivation go beyond the school. One must remember that for every child with a poor self-image in the classroom, there are more than likely two parents at home with the same perception of life. The school cannot go into the home and change the home patterns that have developed over the years, but the school can change its own patterns. The time has come when the school must focus on those elements over which it has control. The teacher is highly significant in this respect, mainly because the teacher plays an important part in the way a child learns if he learns at all.

Thus, the teacher becomes one of the most significant individuals in the life of the culturally deprived child. There is one place in the cultural milieu that pupils may find constant — the classroom. The inner-city, with all of its turmoil and grinding poverty, can provide one haven to which the slum pupil may withdraw from the pointings of society. Within this haven, the type of nurture is dependent upon the teacher and the teaching process.

A pupil's learning is, in a large measure, determined by the attitudes of the teacher. The role of the teacher in the inner-city is a difficult one, for there the teacher must make significant adaptations of style to pupil differences. Making these adaptations requires that the teacher, not only maintain an academic program consistent with the requirements of the school district, but also provide an emotional and ego-supporting environment. This requires the teacher to provide for strong interpersonal relationships between himself and his students.

> The most direct and effective way to strengthen the school as an ego-supporting institution is to improve the interpersonal relationships between teacher and students.[8]

[5] Kvaraceus, *op. cit.*

[6] A. Harry Passow, Editor, Education in Depressed Areas (New York: Bureau of Publications, Teachers College, Columbia University, 1963).

[7] *Ibid.*

[8] Kvaraceus, *op. cit.*, p. 110.

The Community School Director,
Teacher Attitude and The Deprived Child

Philosophically speaking, the relationship between a student and his teacher is essentially a private one. Because of the nature of this relationship and experience, teaching may be considered an art. Kahlil Gibran expresses this concept in a most eloquent fashion in his verse, "On Teaching".

> Then said a teacher, Speak to us of Teaching.
> And he said:
> No man can reveal to you aught but that which already lies half asleep in the dawning of your knowledge.
> The teacher who walks in the shadow of the temple, among his followers, gives not of his wisdom but rather of his faith and his lovingness.
> If he is indeed wise, he does not bid you enter the house of his wisdom, but rather leads you to the threshold of your own mind.
>
> The astronomer may speak to you of his understanding of space, but he cannot give you his understanding. The musician may sing to you of the rhythm which is in all space but he cannot give you the ear which arrests the rhythm nor the voice that echos it. And he who is versed in the science of numbers can tell the regions of weight and measure, but he cannot conduct you thither.
> For the vision of one man lends not its wings to another. And even as each one of you stands alone in God's knowledge, so must each one of you be alone in his knowledge of God and in his understanding of the earth. [9]

The teacher is in a unique relationship to the children in his classroom. On one hand he is the holder of knowledge, but on the other hand, the giver of knowledge. The way it is given becomes one of concernment. For in this artistic relationship, the attitudes of the giver in relation to the receiver are of paramount significance.

Teachers as Models

Research concludes that the disadvantaged need models to emulate. In the inner-city and slum environment there is little beauty to be seen.

---

[9] Kahlil Gibran, *The Prophet* (New York: Knoph Publishing Co., 1929), pp. 56-57.

84

The children have few meaningful relationships with adults. The home provides few opportunities for support and encouragement. Kavaraceus poses the problem of a weak family relationship as a problem to the individual pupil and to the teacher-pupil relationships.

A father who feels defeated by the world is not in a good position to give his son a sense of optimism and a feeling that he can achieve something himself. The fact that the father is most likely to be the absent member of the family and often is replaced by a succession of fathers or father substitutes also tends to militate against the establishment of a view of the male as a reliable, responsible individual. If the boy sees around him men who are unable to sustain a consistent and positive social and economic role, it is hard for the youngster to build a different pattern out of his limited experience.[10]

The school then becomes even more important to these pupils for the school setting becomes a focal point for building self-concept and attitudes that will enable pupils to cope successfully with the problems of learning and living.

David and Pearl Ausubel in their investigations conclude that lack of models, as well as other deprivations, have a debilitating effect on the culturally deprived and particularly Negro pupils.

During pre-adolescence, segregated Negro children characteristically develop low aspirations for academic and vocational achievement. These low aspirations reflect existing social class and ethnic values, the absence of emulatory models, marked educational retardation, restricted vocational opportunities, lack of parental and peer group support, and the cultural impoverishment of the Negro home.[11]

Teacher Attitude Toward Students

The basic assumption is that teacher attitudes are significant for learning. A recent study by Beeman N. Phillips indicates that it is very difficult to measure teacher effectiveness. The teaching process is so complex that it is almost impossible to measure.

[10]Kvaraceus, *op. cit.*, p. 20.

[11]Beeman N. Phillips, "The Individual and The Classroom Group as Frames of Reference in Determining Teacher Effectiveness," *Journal of Educational Research,* Vol. 58 (November, 1964), p. 128.

The outcomes of teaching would be complexly determined by at least four factors: the characteristics of the teacher, the students, the subject matter, and the class as a group. And what is more important, it appears to be the interaction of these factors which partly produces differences in outcomes in teaching.[12]

This complexity militates against finding real answers to the problem of teacher attitudes. The multiplicity of variables within a classroom makes one realize how important the teaching position is, and how critical it becomes when it loses the fineness that comes with the touch of the true artist.

However, there is one recent study that does indicate that teacher attitude is a singular factor in the classroom. A recent study by Heil, Powell and Feifer[13] shows that certain types of teachers get along better with certain types of pupils. The ability to classify teachers and pupils as to types is indicative of the fact that attitudes are recognizable in the classroom environment and that these attitudes do play a significant role.

Riessman[14] is concerned with teacher attitudes when he points out that subtle discrimination does exist in the classroom. Teachers' unfavorable images and expectations militate against the respect and the encouragement so badly needed by the culturally deprived child. He also indicates that school psychologists and counselors frequently underestimate the possibility of the economically underprivileged going to college. Oliver completed a study based upon the stated educational beliefs of 119 elementary teachers, as contrasted with their actual classroom practices. The study was based on four commonly accepted principles of learning.

1. Good teaching recognizes and provides for individual differences among children.

2. Human growth and development is a continuous process.

[12] *Ibid.*, p. 124.

[13] *Ibid.*, p. 124.

[14] F. Riessman, *The Culturally Deprived Child* (New York: Haynes & Brothers, Inc., 1962), p. 36.

3. Real learning is based upon experiencing.

4. Learning proceeds best when related to the interests and experiences of the learner.[15]

To determine to what extent teachers accepted these four principles and the concepts embodied in them, a fifty-item check list of educational beliefs was prepared. The check list revealed that the teachers showed a high degree of acceptance of those beliefs. Evaluation of the teachers showed that there was a wide difference between beliefs and practice. The correlation between belief scores and the evaluation scores was .31, an extremely low correlation indicating practically no relationship.[16]

Oliver came to the following conclusions:

1. Teachers in general have little real understanding of the basic principles of child growth and development.

2. Teachers have not been given the necessary techniques to develop a classroom program based on child needs, interests and capacities.

3. The actual provision for individual differences in most classrooms is very limited.

4. The learning experiences are in many cases, still limited to assignment, recitation type of activity.[17]

Leonard Kronberg supports the conclusions reached above. His observations indicate that teachers have a difficult time in slum schools because the principles they have learned in teaching do not work in their classrooms. Teachers of the culturally deprived use rigorous training, unbending structure, strict discipline, careful avoidance of stimulation and archaic assignment-recitation systems to maintain order. "They (teachers) are bewildered and desperate; they feel they cannot reach these children; they clutch at the teaching choices mentioned (which their own experience and education contradict); they bitterly submit to a "trainer's" role or misguidedly try a

---

[15] W.A. Oliver, "Teachers Educational Beliefs Versus Their Classroom Practices," *Journal of Educational Research,* XLVII (September, 1953), pp. 48-49.

[16] *Ibid.,* p. 53.

[17] *Ibid.,* pp. 54-55.

clinician's role, and they no longer have faith that they can be teachers anymore — in these classrooms."[18]

This gap between what is known and what is actually practiced is a serious problem. Dr. Earl Kelley, in Education For What is Real,[19] mentions the fact that when we know how to teach children and still don't do it we are giving indication that we really don't care.

Attitudes have been defined in various ways. According to Stern there seems to be agreement on at least four points concerning attitudes:

1. Attitudes are socially formed. They are based on cultural experience and training and are revealed in cultural products. The study of life history data reveals the state of mind of the individual and of the social group from which he derives, concerning the values of the society in which he lives.

2. Attitudes are orientations toward others and toward objects.

3. Attitudes are selective. They provide for discrimination between alternative courses of action and introduce consistency of response in social situations of an otherwise diverse nature.

4. Attitudes reflect a disposition to an activity, not a verbalization. They are organizations of incipient activities, of actions not necessarily completed, and represent therefore the underlying dispositional or motivational urge.[20]

These four definitions form a basis for measuring attitudes of teachers. Although measurement is very difficult, much of teacher actions within the classroom can be defined in the terms of these four ideas, for it is evident that attitudes are socially formed, oriented toward others, are selective and reflect in actions toward others.

Miriam L. Goldberg in an abstract from "Adapting Teacher Style to Pupil Differences", dealing with the subject, "Teachers for Disadvantaged

[18] Passow, *op. cit.*, p. 265.

[19] Earl C. Kelley, *Education For What is Real* (New York: Harper and Row Publishers, 1947).

[20] George Stern, "Measuring Noncognitive Variables in Research on Teaching," Handbook of Research on Teaching (Washington, D.C.: National Education Association, 1963), p. 404.

Children", constructs a model teacher for these pupils. This model teacher would have the following attributes:

1. A successful teacher of the disadvantaged is one who respects the children in his classes and they, in turn, respect him; sees these children in his classes quite realistically, views the alien culture of his pupils not as a judge, but as a student, knows that many of the children bear the scars of intellectual understimulation in their early years, knows and understands and has seen the physical conditions under which these children live.

2. The successful teacher of the disadvantaged child meets the child on equal terms, as person to person, individual to individual.[21]

Dr. Goldberg's ideas are concerned with personal and professional attitudes of teachers. Her thinking presents a portrait of a teacher with idealistic overtones. Yet, the culturally deprived children are so severely damaged that the ideal is probably the only answer to the problems these pupils face in the inner-city slums and its environment.

Kvaraceus suggests that the school should become the ego-supporting institution that rebuilds the self-concept of these children. The teacher plays a commanding role in this rebuilding. Thus far, however, there is evidence that the demands made by the school are damaging to these pupils.

> Although the big city systems accept all children, it does so on its own terms. These terms frequently demand some renunciation of differences—personal, social and cultural, and constant submission to the processes of conformity and standardization. Most schools achieve their goals at the prices of some loss of privacy, identity, and individuality . . . . the demands of the large-city school system are most destructive to the egos of the culturally deprived.[22]

"The demands of a large city school system are most destructive to the egos of the culturally deprived."[23] This quotation by Kvaraceus is supported by Clark,[24] Deutsch,[25] and Ausubel.[26]

---

[21] Miriam L. Goldberg, *Mobilization for Youth,* "Adapting Teacher Style to Pupil Differences," March 11, 1963, Abstract (New York: Horace Mann-Lincoln Institute, 1963).

[22] Kvaraceus, *op. cit.,* p. 93.

[23] *Ibid.,* p. 93.

[24] Passow, *op. cit.,* p. 152.

[25] *Ibid.,* p. 177.

[26] *Ibid.,* pp. 118-123.

The Community School Director, Teacher Attitude and The Deprived Child

There is research to prove that the school is not totally to blame for this destruction of the personality, for the home and surrounding environment contribute to it. But, since the school is involved a great deal in human relationships, it is fair to assume that much of the rebuilding of "self" stems from the relationships within the classrooms themselves as indicated by Combs.

Good teachers have always been concerned about individual children and the classroom atmosphere or climate . . . . . These teachers have been concerned with the immediate, with changing ways of seeing things, with bringing knowledge and information to bear on the child's world in such a way that things are seen differently or that new ways of seeing are learned. They know that a good present experience is good for a child no matter what he has to put up with elsewhere. [27]

The positive statements of Combs show that inter-personal relationships between teachers and students are important in attracting and supporting pupils of the inner-city.

Rich ably describes the conflict of teachers attitudes as they relate to teacher-pupil relations within the area of the culturally deprived.

Middle class standards of refinement and ambition mean more to most teachers than many would care to admit, and viewing students through their own middle class perspective, teachers see the world through their own value system. From out of such a system values are placed on the virtues of work, thrift, and cleanliness along with sharply defined standards of respectability, morality, and sexual behavior. But many public school students, coming from a markedly different sociological and socioeconomic background, adhere to a different set of standards. Nor do these students necessarily abhor activities such as dishonesty, sexual promiscuity, unruliness, and carelessness in dress and speech. [28]

Teachers fail to see the real conflict that is present. They fail to recognize the characteristics and social patterns of these pupils.

---

[27] Arthur W. Combs, Chairman *Perceiving, Behaving, Becoming,* (Washington, D.C.: A.S.C.D. Yearbook, National Education Association, 1962), p. 80.

[28] John Rich, "How Social Class Values Affect Teacher Pupil Relations," *The Journal of Educational Sociology,* Vol. 33, (May 1966)

Bettelheim, in an article in the September, 1965, NEA Journal comes to the same conclusions as Rich.

In meeting with teachers of the underprivileged—it became apparent that white and Negro teachers had similar attitudes toward their pupils and that classroom problems were not based on color but grew out of the clash between the teacher's middle class attitudes and their pupil's lower class attitudes. [29]

Bettelheim further observed that these teachers are academic and achievement-oriented rather than oriented to the needs of the individual.

Pressured by this resentment, they concentrate on academic learning and ignore those emotional problems which when not handled, prevent learning altogether. [30]

In concluding the survey of literature and research, there are strong indications that the teacher bears an awesome burden in the classroom. Teacher attitude plays a major role in the learning process. Kvaraceus, writing in the *Negro Self-Concept*, reports that the attitudinal role of the professional staff member is highly significant. "The most direct and effective way to strengthen the school as an ego-supporting institution is to improve the interpersonal relationships between teacher and students." [31]

Riessman concludes that there should be a special type of teacher for the culturally deprived, a teacher with a special type of attitude.

The most successful teachers in terms of the culturally deprived children seem to combine the traditional concepts of structure, order, discipline and strong external demands for achievement with the newer methods of down-to-earth learning by doing. [32]

The attitudes of the teacher in the classroom have a large bearing on classroom success, achievement, and acceptance of the educational process by the pupil. Combs [33] makes a strong plea for teacher attitude to be concerned with the individual child, especially as it relates to failure.

---

[29] Bruno Bettelheim, "Teaching the Disadvantage," *NEA*/p. 356. *Journal*, Vol. 54 (September, 1965), p. 8.

[30] *Ibid.*, p. 11.

[31] Kvaraceus, *op. cit.*, p. 110.

[32] Riessman, *op. cit.*, p. 21.

[33] Combs, *op. cit.*, p. 232.

The Community School Director,
Teacher Attitude and The Deprived Child

Ausubel [34], Sexton [35], Deutsch [36], and Haubrich [37] all conclude that teachers for big-city schools must be of a special kind, have certain attitudes, special training, and develop within themselves a personal philosophy that will meet the needs of these disadvantaged Americans.

No individual in the educational program has a better opportunity to make a difference than a Community School Director. The type of tasks that are required places this individual in a peculiar position, one of a teacher-counselor, friend-coach, model-hero relationship. The nature of the program, one of interest and fun, allows the Director to know the child more intimately and to assist other people within the program to better understand the child and his environment.

From an outside point of view from within, having the privilege of both worlds, the Director can help change attitudes, of both children and adults, and particularly teachers. This philosophy is encompassed in the words of Gibran when he says, "gives not of his wisdom, but rather of his faith and his lovingness." [38]

[34] Passow, *op. cit.*, pp. 109-141.

[35] Patricia Sexton, *Education and Income* (New York: Viking Press, Inc., 1961).

[36] Passow, *op. cit.*, pp. 163-180.

[37] *Ibid.*, pp. 243-261.

[38] Gibran, *op. cit.*, p. 56.

CHAPTER VI

**THE COMMUNITY SCHOOL DIRECTOR
AND
COMMUNITY INTEREST GROUPS**

The Community School Director
and Community Interest Groups

The Community School Director works within an environment where the school is just one of the influences bringing pressure to bear upon the various issues in a community. The school in no sense of the word can be isolated. The school can be understood only when it is seen in relation to other agencies within the total society. These agencies in many instances are interest groups, and the school cannot ignore how they are organized; why they are organized nor by whom they are operated.

Hunter indicates there are four community groups with which the schools must contend, and these groups have certain goals they strive for in their reach for power. These include:

1. Business groups.

2. Government groups.

3. Civic association.

4. Society activities.[1]

---

[1] Floyd Hunter, *Community Power Structure* (Chapel Hill, N.C., 1953).

The educational institution has been what sociologists would call a reflective or adaptive institution. Big business and big government are pivotal or formative institutions. Though they may work hard behind the scenes, and do not send official delegates to the board of education to pound on the tables, it is their decisions and wishes which are most influential in all that is vital in the directions of society.[2]

The Director of a Community School must recognize there exists within the community a dichotomous relationship between what people express in terms of democratic beliefs and what really does exist. In our society we believe the schools are free from outside pressures, but in reality they are not. It must also be recognized that these outside influences may be of value and service in developing a Community School Program. In fact, if many of these influential structures do not support the schools and the programs adopted to further an improvement in the social climate of a given community, not much will be accomplished.

Knowing that this exists is not enough. The Community School Director must relate these outside forces to what is happening in the school and develop working relationships between himself and these various sources of influence. These interrelationships are essential to continual growth.

This may sound as if there is a suggestion that a Community School Director, may by some stretch of the imagination, be involved in politics. If one is to take a narrow view of this term, then it would not be true except in the sense that the individual has certain basic citizenship rights. But if the word politics is to be used in a broad context, then a Community School Director has a definite interest in politics.

The term "politics" need not—and should not—be viewed as confined to narrow conceptions of shady deals, unscrupulous patronage activity, or other forms of unprofessional conduct. Instead of viewing politics as something unsavory or disreputable, it should be perceived as a necessary procedure for making decisions in a democracy.

The studies of community power structure have demonstrated that education is, and indeed ought to be, in politics.[3]

---

[2] Kerber, August and Wiefred Smith, *Educational Issues in a Changing Society*, (Wayne State University Press, Detroit, Michigan, 1964) ,p. 278.

[3] Edgar O. Morphet and Charles O. Ryan, *Planning and Effecting Needed Changes in Education* (Eight State Project, Denver, Colorado, June 1967), p. 116.

Kimbrough in the same article lists the following power systems within a community that are of concern to those in education.

Sector	Position of Person Most Frequently Used for Sector
1. News Media	Newspaper editor and publishers
2. Banking and Finance	Bank president of large bank
3. Business	Owners of large business
4. Health	Physicians
5. Chamber of Commerce	President or executive director
6. Law	Outstanding lawyer in community
7. Women	Women active in social activities[4]

The following should be added to this list to make it more inclusive:

1. Radio and Television Media	Manager or presidents of local broadcast outlet
2. Recreation Department	Director of department or board president
3. Welfare Department	Director of department of social welfare
4. Department of Public Employment	Director of office of employment
5. Juvenile Courts	Juvenile court judge or judges
6. Police Department	Chief of Police
7. Urban Renewal	Director
8. Model Cities	Director
9. Fire Department	Fire chief or station house captain

[4] *Ibid.*, p. 128.

10. Settlement Houses	Director or president of the board
11. Churches	Pastor or priest
12. Parochial Schools	Principal
13. Service Clubs	President
14. Character Building Agencies	Executive Director
15. United Fund Campaign Headquarters	Executive Director
16. Little League Groups	President or coaches

This list is not complete, nor could it ever be, largely since some agencies are indigenous to certain communities. However, the above list indicates the multitude of groups that a Community School Director has access to in the day-to-day operations within a school.

The Community School will always face the need to work with outside groups. The Community School concept is recognized as an institution that cares about the total neighborhood in its broadest sense and translates this concern into action. This is not possible without becoming involved with all groups within the community that wield either political or social power.

A school that involves all the sources of community action would look something like this:

1. A school would be built whose facilities would be available for use by social agencies, health agencies, and interested citizen groups on a seven-days-a-week, twelve-months-a-year basis.

2. The staffs of every agency involved would find new and significant roles to play in a number of new settings.

3. Much closer cooperation would result between schools and agencies.

4. Public agency support would be strongly felt by social workers from the voluntary agencies.

5. Fuller sharing of data would be facilitated.

6. There would be a neighborhood base of operations for many centralized agencies.

98

7. Closer contacts among citizens and agencies would ensue.

8. Preventive problems could more easily be launched.

9. Each institution could establish a closer tie with its neighborhood.

10. A climate of mutual interest among agencies would aid the trial of new programs.

11. Through closer contact with many institutions and agencies, professionals would broaden their understanding and develop more generalized skills than heretofore. Thus a new breed of generalists might arise among social workers. This could correct the atomizing effects of the overspecialization now evident.

12. Opportunities would open for observation of and communication with children and adults in a wide variety of situations.

13. All workers would come to have a neighborhood "bias" rather than an agency bias.[5]

CHARACTERISTICS OF ORGANIZATIONS

A Community School Director needs to have some basic information concerning organizations within the community in which he works. It is fairly easy to learn the names, the addresses and some of the purposes of almost any group. This is not enough.

Organizations, small and large, have particular characteristics that are applicable in nearly every case. These include:

1. The larger the community, the more the organizations.

2. The more differentiated the community, the more groupings that will be organized to take care of these various groupings, such as social, ethnic, religious, residence, etc.

3. Organizations tend to develop other organizations. One group organized around an issue may well cause the development of a group opposed to this point of view.

---

[5] Henry Saltzman, "The Community School in the Urban Setting," from Passow, A. Harry, *Education in Depressed Areas* (New York: Teachers College Press, 1963), pp. 327-328.

4. Groups that are brought together on a voluntary basis tend to become formalized.

5. Non-profit organizations often lose their major purposes and lose their non-profit status.

6. The larger the organization, the more people involved and the more difficult it is to get answers or decisions.

7. The less formal the group, the less power it has.

8. The more bureaucratic a group is, the less chance there is for implementation of change. [6]

The preceding are general and may be fairly obvious. However, these ideas are basic to working with outside agencies. For example: Item 8 says that, "The more bureaucratic a group is, the less chance there is for implementation of change." With this knowledge, a Community School Director will know that it will be rather difficult to work with the Department of Social Welfare. A family in need of instant aid will probably not be helped by either sending them or going with them to this agency. The rules of this agency are tightly structured, and aid is given for a particular reason at specified times. This is a departmental rule and enforced by a myriad of laws and regulations. Also, since it is a very large organization, the decision-making process is labyrinthian. Knowing this, a Community School Director, in working with a family in dire need, would choose an alternative to the Welfare Department. Knowing these problems, over a period of time a Community School Director would develop several alternatives for solving problems, using various agencies at various times in order to make prompt decisions relating to critical issues.

WORKING WITH INTEREST GROUPS

Communicating with groups is one of the most important jobs that a Community School Director has. In fact, unless this happens, the program stays within the school building and there is no Community School. As a director plans to develop a program, it is essential that various groups within the community become a part and parcel of the decision making process.

[6] Bernard Berelson and Gary A. Steiner, *Human Behavior, An Inventory of Scientific Findings,* (New York: Harcourt, Brace and World, Inc., 1964), Chapter 9.

Money, taxation, program support, new program development, community involvement all depend on the ability of the individual director to communicate with a network of interrelated agencies and with various large and small groups in the community.

BANKING, FINANCE AND BUSINESS

Education is good for business. This has long been recognized by the National Chamber of Commerce and other related agencies. Joseph Anderson, former vice-president of General Motors writes:

> Unfortunately, often hardest to convince or the most indifferent are the business people of the community. I was one of them. Businessmen seldom appreciate or even understand what better education for people means to their business success. As an example, not too many years ago in Atlanta the per capita spending for the public schools was the lowest of any major city in the United States. At the time, the people in Atlanta were very proud of their low tax rate, and the Chamber of Commerce used this fact to entice new business to town.

> Exasperated, the superintendent of schools finally hit on the idea of doing some comparative research in business statistics—comparing Atlanta with other cities. The results of his research showed that, while Atlanta had the lowest cost per child in the public schools, Atlanta also had the lowest annual spending per capita in the retail business.

> Furthermore, his research developed a close correlation between per capita spending for education and the per capita retail business in any city. So, the cities that showed a high per capita spending for schools also showed a high per capita spending in retail business.[7]

To understand and to know the Banking and Business Industry within a community means that the Director must know the people involved and to understand the way they think. This means that the Director has to get out,

---

[7] Joseph A. Anderson, "The Economic Value of the Community School Concept to Local Business," *The Community School and Its Administration*, May 1969.

meet people and capitalize on contacts. These contacts cannot be made sitting in a building. The Director needs to develop a systematic program of education for the business community. There needs to be a method of communication through talks, news letters, local media, membership in service clubs, and through committee involvement so these members of the community power structure have the opportunity to apprise themselves of the value of Community Education to them, not only personally but in an economic way. Anderson continues when he writes:

> Yet, I told the young Community School Director in Guadua-lupe: "You have a potential market of $6,000,000 per year for Phoenix businessmen. If each of these 1,000 families could earn an income of $6,000 a year, which is average to many families, they would have $6,000,000 a year to spend for cars, houses, furniture, TV, and what not. This is a plan that your business community should be eager to help you achieve."[8]

The business community needs to be educated to understand that poor people make poor business. People that are undereducated and under-employed really are economic liabilities rather than assets and represent red ink to a businessman.

> Business is people, but the thousands of people who live in the shacks in the Carolinas or Arizona or elsewhere, with no sanitary facilities, no furniture, diseased children, are not good customers. No use for anyone to go into business for these people.[9]

CHARACTER BUILDING AGENCIES

Within many communities there will be a large number of these organizations. Some of the better known ones will be the Y.M.C.A., the Y.W.C.A., the Boy and Girl Scouts, the Campfire Girls, 4-H Clubs, etc. All of these appear to be in competition with the schools. They offer many opportunities for recreation, provide clubs, sponsor enrichment activities and in some instances offer educational programs for remediation. The Community School concept often offers a threat, for they see the schools open and their

[8] *Ibid.*

[9] *Ibid.*

own facilities closing. They also see the Community School being supported by a constant income from public taxes while their organization must fight for every nickel from a fickle public. The school can plan, can budget and program without too much concern about the next dollar, whereas their programs face a hand to mouth existence.

In the film, "To Touch a Child," this is often mentioned. Doesn't this program kill the various agencies that are now working within a community?

First, in many communities, there are not too many of these services available. The Community School can step into the vacuum and provide programs of this nature.

Secondly, in communities where there are these services, there is documented evidence to indicate that these agencies prosper even more when the Community School is developed. This comes about because of two reasons:

1. More services require more services. As people become interested and involved, they tend to want more involvement. Their interests broaden and they see the need for a wider variety of activities.

2. As the Community School concept becomes accepted, the economic climate of the community improves. As more discretionary income is made available, these agencies share in the excess.

A Community School Director will be able to relate to these various agencies by:

1. Getting to know the people in the programs.

2. Serving on various boards that represent these agencies.

3. Contributing time and leadership to their programs.

4. Encouraging them to use the public school facilities.

5. Suggesting to them the development of new programs in neighborhoods and providing services that are not now available.

6. Using their buildings when the schools cannot provide adequate physical facilities.

7. Giving them credit for providing a very valuable service within the community.

8. Helping these agencies to find leadership for their activities.

9. Encouraging constituents to use the services of these agencies.

CHURCHES AND PAROCHIAL SCHOOLS

Within every community there will be churches of various denominations. In some, there will be schools. The Community School Program can aid these institutions. Again, the Director needs to know the various people involved in the groups. The ministers, the rabbis, the priests, the principals and teachers in the schools should become familiar as friends. These people are part of the warp and woof of the community and deserve recognition for the influence they have in making the community a better place in which to live.

The Director needs to meet with these people and understand their concerns and problems. The programs they offer are important, and can add to the quality of life in a community.

One of the most pressing issues with these groups is that many of them feel that outside programs offered by the Community Schools compete with their programs. A second area of potential conflict is in the use of facilities. The churches often need facilities, particularly athletic facilities, for use by their youth. Also, many parochial schools have limited athletic facilities in such areas as indoor tracks, tennis courts, swimming pools and large stadia.

The Community School Director can work with these agencies in the following ways:

1. Know the leadership.

2. Offer to work with them in their programs.

3. Eliminate as many conflicts as possible by checking with the leadership before making plans for new programs and scheduling events.

4. Share facilities where possible and when the law does not conflict.

5. Make certain that all Community School programs are open to all citizens in the community and that information concerning these programs is made available.

104

6. Hold regular meetings with the leadership of these groups to plan and to inform.

7. Encourage them to take part in the Community School program.

JUVENILE POLICE DEPARTMENT

Juvenile delinquency is a problem in nearly every community. This social problem taints the moral climate of the community and weakens the moral fiber of the members of society. Prevention is the surest cure, with education running a close second. A Community School Director is in a unique position in that he can work in both areas.

Prevention is assured when the school and home work together with the Juvenile Department in developing programs that provide youngsters with meaningful activities. An example of this type of cooperation is in a city in California where the Police and the Schools, along with the Recreation Department, sponsored a boy's band, with uniforms, leadership and a program of practice, parades and travel. This band enrolled, for the most part, impoverished and deprived boys. The school district provided the uniforms and busses for transportation. The schools gave leadership in teaching and direction. The Police Department provided leadership and supervision. The Recreation Department provided supervision, leadership and some financial aid. Community members provided money and backing. Many youngsters, who would otherwise be left out on the streets, had a program sponsored by adults in the community. Real, live, meaningful models were available for young boys who would not otherwise have had positive relationships with outstanding men in the community. Besides having a good program for adolescents, the Police themselves were cast in a very favorable light.

A Community School Director can work with the Juvenile Department in many ways. Some of them might include:

1. Getting to know those in responsible positions within the department.

2. Planning with them for programs that they see a need for in the community.

3. Keeping posted on the problems that the police see in the various neighborhoods.

4. Providing them with information concerning problems in the neighborhood and community.

105

5. Using these individuals in a very positive manner whenever possible by bringing them into the schools to speak, to work and to be a member of the education team.

JUVENILE COURTS

There is no possible way that a Community School Director can prevent some youngsters from getting into trouble. When this does happen, the Community School Director should become involved with the juvenile court system. Many youngsters will not have an advocate in court, largely because they do not have one at home. This can be an important role for any Community School Director. This will mean:

1. The Community School Director must be familiar with the Juvenile Court System in his community.

2. The Community School Director must know personally the juvenile judges.

3. The Community School Director must know the process whereby he can become an advocate.

4. The Community School Director must know and be able to call on legal aid when necessary.

In a community in California the school principal, because the nature of his position and the school in which he served required it, contacted a neighborhood lawyer for services when needed. This lawyer gave his advice, without pay, largely because he himself was interested and was impressed with the concern of the school official. This is not unusual. Many professional members in a community will do this. They only wait to be asked, which is typical in a normal community. The difference in a community where the Community School concept is at work is that these people will become volunteers.

The Community School Director can help children and their families in several ways. Many times the juvenile will be remanded back to the family on the recommendation of the Director. In other instances, the youngster may be given a warning and the Director is to be placed in a counseling situation. At other times, probation will be passed as a sentence, and the Director will work with the probation officer. In any instance, the child is the important figure in this process and in each instance, the Community School Director can play a major role.

106

COMMUNICATIONS MEDIA

We live in a world that bombards our senses with a constant flow of information. Someone has referred to this as our "modern day sensory overload." In every geographical area of our corporate life there are radio stations, television stations and newspapers. These media are essential to providing our protean society with the necessary information for day to day living. The people involved in providing these processes are looking for news. Education, no matter what its shape or style, is newsworthy. This places the Community School in the vortex of public view, for this is where much of the action is.

A Community School Director must be cognizant of the various media and plan ways of using these to his best advantage as well as just providing a news outlet.

The following should be given consideration in working with the various media in a community:

1. Get to know the people involved in the media business.

2. Cooperate with them in all instances.

3. Call them before something is going to happen.

4. Use them whenever possible.

5. Send written information to them about new programs.

6. Invite them to be participants in all events.

7. Provide space, services and courtesy to them.

8. Be liberal with free passes and other gratuities.

9. Give them credit for their services.

10. Ask them to help with your own information services.

A Community School Director develops good relations with the local newspaper or other media to a point that the schools may be encouraged to provide news for the various media on a sustaining basis. In Newton, Iowa, the new school superintendent wasted little time in making contacts with the local paper. The result was that they asked him to write a weekly column called the "Supergram". In this column, Dr. Congreve is able to provide news to the local citizens concerning education in the community. Two of these columns follow. The first deals with the purposes of establishing individual school committees in order to bring the schools and the community closer together in the educational process.

Committee Can Unite School Staff, Citizens

Supergram

By W. J. Congreve

Two weeks ago I described the several committees which are being formed to bring the Newton Community School District staff and the citizens of Newton closer together. Today, I would like to visit with you about the community program advisory committees.

Most professionals realize that separation between themselves and their clients can have serious effects upon the outcome of their work. As part of their general practice, they ask the client to report on how well he is getting along. These reports are then used to help the professional decide whether the program he has designed or the method he is using is producing the desired effects. These people realize that unless they can learn what effect they are having upon their client, they run the risk of loosing that client or not having others come to them.

Public school educators do not usually do this. They operate a kind of monopoly. Regardless of how badly a school is functioning, it is rarely put out of business. Many educators do not seem to realize that great benefits can accrue by asking their clients to tell them what they think about school programs. Some teachers behave as if they possess a supernatural power. They tell parents not to interfere, that teachers always know what is best.

In Newton, we are most fortunate. The gap between the schools and the community is not very wide. Parents often feel free to make suggestions. What seems to be needed is a procedure whereby children and parents can systematically review school programs and make constructive suggestions for improvements.

The community program advisory committees will serve this function. Representative parents from every grade level, along with children from the intermediate, upper and secondary school levels, will meet with representative teachers and the principal once each month to examine the various elements of their school's program. Each school committee will determine its own study agenda. One school's committee may begin with the reading program; another may focus on the recess program or the lunch program.

The topic for the next meeting will always be established one month in advance. This will allow time for each member to talk with people whom he represents to gather information needed for a fruitful discussion.

We do not expect that all aspects of each school will be considered during any one year. Our schools are complex organizations; it is quite possible that some areas may never be considered by a committee.

The community program advisory committees will not be used to settle personal gripes and complaints. If these come up, the individuals concerned will be invited to talk directly to the principal or the staff members concerned.

The community program advisory committee to the superintendent will examine district-wide programs and policies. It will also welcome problems which parents or children feel are not being adequately discussed in a local principal's committee. Again, the topic for each meeting will be established in advance to give members time to gather ideas, formulate questions and develop suggestions.

One might say that our community program advisory committees will be conducting market research for our school district. I want to assure the citizens of Newton that the comments, criticisms and recommendations which come out of these committees will be used in redesigning school programs and in upgrading teaching methodology.

"Come, let us reason together. We need your assistance."

The second deals with the problem of closing school during inclement weather. It takes the public into the decision-making process and explains the problems inherent in making decisions. In this case, the superintendent treats the public as if they are intelligent, capable people, with a legitimate right to know and to understand the nature of such a problem. It is a fine example of allowing the community the right to know, to be informed.

Closing School On Bad Day

Supergram

By W. J. Congreve

Bad weather may soon be upon us; decisions to close school may be required. I should like to describe how the superintendent of schools makes this difficult decision.

Before retiring each evening, I make sure my telephone is right next to me. Then I will hear it at 5:30 a.m. should Lyle Blum, our transportation supervisor, call. Blum is responsible for keeping our buses running. At the same time he must maintain the safest conditions for our children.

Blum gets up at 3:30 a.m. to check the weather. If there is any indication that some roads may be impassable due to snow, ice, sleet or fog, he gets into his car immediately and checks the entire bus route to make sure the buses can operate safely. He is especially concerned about ice and fog. These conditions are treacherous; they can be local and appear unexpectedly.

The Iowa School Code requires that classes be held only when all students have a way to school. Therefore, Blum must make sure that arrangements can be made to pick up all bused students. When Blum finishes his tour, he calls me to report. This usually occurs about 5:30 a.m. If there is any question, Blum comes to my home to discuss the problem and make recommendations.

One might think that after this inspection the decision to close or keep open the schools would be very simple. Unfortunately, it is not. Buses do not begin to operate until 7:15 a.m. Many changes in the weather and road conditions can take place between 5:30 and 7:15. They can become much better, or they can become much worse. Moreover, many activities, such as preparation for lunches, must begin at 6:30 a.m.

We are always primarily concerned for the safety of our children; yet the schools must be open so many days each year. Three days are included in our school calendar to cover weather emergencies. If the schools must close for more than three days, additional days must be added during the spring months to make up the time lost.

Taking all of these matters into consideration, I finally come to a decision. At 6 a.m. I telephone radio stations KCOB, KGRN and WHO which have agreed to broadcast this decision to parents and children.

I hope that there will not be many mornings when I am called upon to make this difficult decision. I suspect occasionally my decision will not appear to be the best one in the eyes of some people. However, I hope that everyone will realize the uncertainties involved and the difficulty of predicting what will happen to the weather.

A good Community School will publish some type of a newspaper or newsletter at regular intervals. This should be developed by the Director for informational purposes. The work in most cases will be done by someone else, although the purpose of this material is to promote the program and inform the constituents concerning the Community School.

When developing a school newsletter, remember to:

1. Make an attractive newsletter, printed when possible.

2. Set high quality standards.

3. Be accurate in reporting.

4. Use names whenever possible. People like to see their names in print.

5. Ask for help from the various media.

6. Make sure that the principal is involved.

7. Mail copies to every home rather than distribute through the children.

8. Keep the news brief and to the point.

9. Never editorialize.

RECREATION DEPARTMENT

As in all political subdivisions, there is often a duplication of programs. This is not necessarily bad, since in a non-linear society there is room for a wide range of services to provide for an equally broad range of interests.

The Community School provides a great deal of recreation. There is more than just a chance that a Recreation Department may feel that the Community School is in competition with it and as a result may feel threatened. After showing the film "To Touch a Child" to a group of public officials brought together by a mayor in a midwestern city, the college professor making the presentation was accosted by a recreation director following the showing and publicly criticized for wanting to establish a program in the community that would essentially destroy the Recreation Department. This destruction would mean that many would lose their jobs as well as a great deal of power. There was also the criticism that a large public investment in recreational facilities would be eliminated.

This is a fairly typical reaction, particularly from those who do not understand the total concept of community education. Perhaps, too, the presentation was not as good as it might have been.

All of the evidence that is in at the present time indicates that the Community School Program enhances the recreation program in a community. Playgrounds, parks, camping areas, ice-skating rinks, picnic areas and public boating facilities are used more in communities where there is such a program in operation than in communities without.

The cooperation between the recreation department and the schools is increased. There is better planning of programs because they work together. Facilities are planned with each in mind. An example of this planning may be found in some cities on the West Coast. There the schools and the recreation departments jointly plan a new school site. The playground is really part of the park. The swimming pool is placed on the school grounds. There the schools can use the parks and the pool during the school hours. When the schools close in the afternoon, the recreation department runs the program on the school grounds. There is a sharing of expenses. The taxpayers benefit by not duplicating expensive facilities. There is a sharing in the expenses of landscaping and maintenance. This saves on manpower, equipment, fencing, and the like. A Community School Program is a cooperative program, where all agencies that serve are given a chance to work within the limits of their capabilities. A Community School Program is not concerned with who does it, only that it gets done in the most efficient manner and that people benefit.

In working with the Recreation Department it is well to remember to:

1. Get to know the people who run the department.
2. Become familiar with their programs.

3. Never duplicate a program unless absolutely necessary.

4. Plan with them when new programs are being considered.

5. Allow them to do those things at which they are best suited.

6. Encourage their use of school facilities.

7. Involve them personally in the schools' activities.

8. Provide leadership for their programs from the school staff.

9. Attend their functions and commend them for their activities.

10. Support them in their efforts to extend their programs.

11. Share in the use of equipment. Work out satisfactory ways in which they can use the school equipment and the schools can share the equipment provided by the recreation department.

SERVICE CLUBS

In every community there will be a number of service clubs that will have some influence on life in that community. These organizations can be a well-spring of good will. They are organized around the concept of service. A major role of a Community School Director is to work with these various groups in developing an increased consciousness of quality in defining community service. Many of the activities that are carried out by luncheon clubs tend to be rather shallow. There is almost always room for improvement.

In working with such groups, it has been found that the following should be considered:

1. Get involved in at least one club, preferably more.

2. Visit other clubs and talk about the program. The great impetus given to the Community Education Program began at a Rotary Club luncheon in 1935.

3. Ask these clubs to help.

4. Provide them with suggestions for service projects.

5. Invite them into the school to hold their meetings. The cafeteria can provide the luncheon. The students can provide the program.

6. Encourage other people in the school system to join.

7. Give these groups recognition.

8. Mention these clubs in the news letter.

9. Work with them on their special projects.

10. Provide them with student groups for programs at special times during the year, such as Christmas, Thanksgiving, etc.

At a high school in the far West, a Kiwanis Club came into a high school and worked with the school establishing a senior high school Key Club. Adult members sponsored the students. Each high school member thus had an adult friend, counselor and advocate. This senior club became interested in vandalism and took on the responsibility of directing a clean campus campaign for the whole community. As this interest lagged, a new project concerning scholarships became important. Along with this, they developed a high school citizen-of-the-month award. Twice each year this club had their noon meeting in the high school. The high school provided the program. This increased the school-club involvement. Both groups benefited.

This one liaison led to other community groups' becoming involved. The Lions Club in the area, not to be outdone, took over the athletic banquet. The club members sponsored individual athletes.

The Rotary Club became interested and held two meetings each year at the school. Again, they were able to be of service in the form of scholarship grants.

In all instances, the school actively solicited the services and the involvement of these individuals. As the senior club members became more interested, they became more involved. The more involved they became, the more influence they had on improving the school situation for many of the young people in attendance.

WELFARE DEPARTMENT

Probably one of the most difficult areas in which to work as a Community School Director is in the area of institutionalized social welfare. This department is so circumscribed by a complicated legal structure that at times it is almost impenetrable. Experience has shown that the best way to work with this bureaucratic organization is to:

1. Get to know those people working within the organization.

2. Become acquainted with the case workers in the neighborhood.

3. Work with the organization in planning educational programs.

4. When the opportunity presents itself, provide in-service experiences for the employees.

5. Cooperate with the department whenever possible.

6. Support them in their contacts whenever feasible.

7. Refer cases to them through regular channels.

8. Involve them in community planning.

In urban areas the Department of Social Welfare becomes an important adjunct of the school. There will be attendance centers where half of the children could be recipients of welfare. Because of this, the contacts made with this governmental group will be of importance, not only to the Community School Director making the contact but also to the students in the school. Improved relations between the school and the welfare organization can benefit everyone.

A principal in California was concerned with the care given to children in a family. Because he knew that the family was on welfare, and because the contacts with the welfare agency were positive, the counseling services of the case worker were available. A visit by the case worker and the principal made a distinct impression on the home. The level of child care improved markedly. This is only one instance and one example.

An assistant superintendent in the same district worked with the Director of Social Welfare to develop various courses to be offered mothers on A.F.D.C. (Aid to Families with Dependent Children). It was agreed that courses in food preparation, clothing repair and alteration, child health, and budget planning were necessary. Attendance at classes improved when the checks were distributed at the school. Although this practice is questionable, there is reason to believe that it has some merit. The important thing in this activity is not to be measured in terms of the payments but to be evaluated by the closeness of cooperation between the schools and the Welfare Department. This agency recognized that it received full consideration. As a result, the

115

principle of community involvement was given full credence and educational support was assured. The schools had helped the Welfare Department do a better job. Their position in the community was enhanced. People were given a chance to improve their skills. The schools provided a real service. This is Community Education.

WOMEN'S ORGANIZATIONS

Without exception in this land in every village, hamlet, town or city there are a variety of women's organizations. They are grouped together for various purposes, some educational, some philanthropic, some social and some for rather nebulous reasons. Nevertheless, they do exist and are within the social structure of the community.

These groups can be a fine source of leadership, school support and financial help. They often need to be cultivated, largely because they tend to isolate themselves from the ongoing activities of the community. Much of their good work goes unnoticed. This is something that needs correction.

A principal in a community on the Pacific Coast once had a problem in finding enough money to provide needy students with help in taking college board examinations and for filing applications to various colleges. In the high school, there was a large number of students unable to take the regular college board examinations because of the examination fee required. Along with this, in many instances students who were capable could not file for scholarships because the colleges and universities required application fees. These fees were not refundable. Students from poor circumstances could not see sending money and not receiving something in return. The risk was too high. In other cases, the students just couldn't find the amount necessary. By chance, the principal and a few of the students were asked to a most influential women's club, the principal to speak about public education in the community and the students to provide the entertainment.

In the discussion that followed the presentation, the school official talked about the problem of student need. At that meeting, this group voted to give the school $800 for aid to needy students and to replenish this whenever it fell below $400. The effect on the school was miraculous. It now had a way to provide all the needy students with the opportunity to receive educational grants, take tests, file for scholarships and to pay for college applications. The end result was that this school that had in 1959-60 received something like $7,000.00 in scholarships increased its grants to over $100,000.00 in 1964-65. There were other factors involved in this increase, but a large part of the increase came about because every student now had an opportunity

116

to compete on an equal basis. This could not have happened without this gift from this women's club.

In working with such groups, one should follow many of the practices found successful in working with service clubs, but with an emphasis on getting to know them. This will take time on the part of the Community School Director.

CHAPTER VII

THE COMMUNITY SCHOOL DIRECTOR AND FISCAL RESPONSIBILITY

The Community School Director and Fiscal Responsibility

INTRODUCTION

A school system may develop a sound educational philosophy that acknowledges the right of every individual to reach his full participation in an open society, but this philosophy may lose much of its impact in implementation because of the educational financing process. If schools are to achieve high quality levels, then there must be a direct relationship between the beliefs concerning education and the dollar resources for the support of education. The American society will find it increasingly difficult to continue to give National Defense, the Vietnam War, and the military-industrial complex priority over those things in its national life that will sustain and develop a quality of life in keeping with its avowed purposes.

In essence, the financing of education must become a real factor in the philosophical base of the educational system. Whereas previously finance has been a major problem only in terms of budgeting, and has seemed to play a rather insignificant role in the social development and the social reconstruction of our society, this must be turned about and a much broader definition of school finance should be recognized.

In the future this will mean a major shift in definition and purpose. School finance will be defined in terms of program rather than in terms of just a tax base and what it costs the individual taxpayer.

The community school concept has a large role to play in the development of this new concept. The role of educational leadership will be significant in changing fiscal definitions. This will come about because there is a definite relationship between the amount spent on education and the total well-being of society in general.

> There is an intimate relationship between schooling and the economic wealth of a nation and its citizens. Prosperity demands productivity, and productivity demands trained talent. Education develops the intellectual and manual skills which underlie the productive abilities of individuals in nations today. Nations with the highest general level of education are those with the highest economic development. Schools, even more than natural resources, are the basis of prosperity.[1]

It is questionable that this concept can be ignored any longer. The loss of manpower because of the inability of the schools to provide adequate programs for all people is a national disgrace. When a fourth of the black men between the ages of 18 and 25 are unemployed, then the potential for revolt and riot is self evident. The force for evil is so great that society cannot but recognize the profound influence that the under-educated have on the social system, and this system must begin to take immediate steps to remedy the situation, if for no other reasons than for mere survival.

How well our society meets the challenge of providing equal educational opportunity to every citizen will rest in its ability to implement with hard dollars the philosophical statements that have been developed over the last two hundred years. Concomitant to this is the willingness of the nation to assign education its proper role as a natural resource. Ultimately, education becomes one of the essential values of our society and the problem of fiscal support becomes one of commitment to one of those values.

The community school director must become familiar with the financing of education and be able to develop budgets that reflect both the fiscal needs and the philosophical concerns of education as conceptualized in community education.

---

[1] National Education Association and American Association of School Administrators, Educational Policies Commission. *National Policy and the Financing of the Public Schools.* Washington, D.C. The Association, 1959, p. 7-9.

THE COMMUNITY SCHOOL DIRECTOR AND FISCAL RESPONSIBILITY

The local district has the main responsibility for developing a financing program. However, it is often difficult for traditionally oriented school boards to see the need for developing school budgets that reflect the community school concept. "It just hasn't been done that way before, so why should we do it now?" Too, there is a fear that the programs will add large amounts of additional money to the program and thus be in conflict with the prudential principle of keeping taxes as low as possible.

There is not a great deal that the local community school director can do about changing the budgetary concepts of the total community except in that as the community education program develops, there is a chance to sell the program to the people. They in turn then put political pressure on the hierarchial structure to evaluate its position concerning school financing.

As the community education program becomes more widely recognized as a viable alternative to more traditional educational programs, there will be more financing available from both state and federal levels. Michigan has already taken a step toward providing financing for districts with these programs. The Federal Government has also recognized the need for community involvement in the Elementary Secondary Education Act of 1965 and in the Office of Economic Opportunity Programs.

Financing by way of these programs is limited in terms of money available and the requirement for a great deal of time in writing basic proposals that meet certain criteria. It is difficult to develop a full-blown program on this type of financing.

Today, many programs are getting started by the "consortium method." A group of interested citizens, school personnel, business men and others join together to encourage the local district to develop a pilot program with the help of outside financing.

An example is a program now in the developmental stage in a midwest community. The school district, after being prodded by a professor from the local university, took serious note of the community education possibilities. At the same time, a Mayor's Task Force on education became interested. Using this action committee as a base of power, other groups were involved: a Community Action Committee, a midwest community college, the Chamber of Commerce, the State Department of Instruction. All of these groups were able to convince the local district of the feasibility of developing a pilot project in one junior high school. The financing of the program came from the following sources.

Source	Funds
Community Action Groups	$ 8,000.00
Community College	5,000.00
University	5,000.00
State Department of Instruction	2,000.00
Local School District	2,500.00
Total	$22,500.00

The Task Force sent the new school director to Flint, Michigan for a six-week training program. After returning to the midwest, the new director was placed in a junior high school to begin developing a program. This could not have come about without the involvement of several groups in helping the school district face a problem of financing a new program.

The budget for the first year included:

Staff salary for director $14,500.00
Program supplies and materials. 3,000.00
Hourly employee expenses 3,500.00
Extra custodial costs 1,500.00

This is a very simple budget. In the future, the director will be responsible for planning a much more complete and complex budget that will give more than an approximation of costs.

Designing a Budget

The community educational director plans the budget with the principal. Early in the school year, plans are formulated for the next fiscal year. In fact, budget planning should be a continuous process. It is recommended that the director plan a preliminary budget that should include the following:

1. Salaries, director
2. Salaries, part time (clerical, secretarial, part-time teachers)
3. Salaries, hourly employees
4. Instructional materials
5. Supplies and equipment
6. Maintenance and custodial services
7. General expenses (telephone, postage, etc.)

8. Mileage for staff
9. Insurance
10. Capital outlay

Most school districts use a uniform accounting procedure. In planning a budget, the director would, of course, use these procedures in the development of a financial plan.

There is no standard amount or percentage that can be considered in planning a program budget for a community school. The budgets are as variable and different as the schools, the programs and the directors. Each community is a separate entity, having special needs. One school program may include a large number of evening courses. Some districts may offer these courses free while others may charge fixed or sliding fees.

In budget planning, the following principles should be given consideration:

1. Do assemble data as soon as possible in the school year.

2. Do work with the principal in planning.

3. Do use past budgets only as guides rather than iron-clad rules.

4. Do work with citizens in planning the budgets. Budgets should reflect the needs of the community and participation is necessary to find these needs.

5. Do develop a preliminary budget early and receive citizen approval.

6. Do present the preliminary budget to the principal and other authorities for review and suggestions.

7. Do revise the preliminary budget in light of recommendations made by school authorities and citizens.

8. Do put the budget in final form for approval.

9. Do publish the budget for all to see.

10. Do stay within the published budget when making expenditures.

Administering the Budget

In a majority of school districts the individual principal or community school director will have little to do with the actual disbursement of money. This is usually done through the central office using the established methods of the district. The community school director must follow the established practices carefully and to the letter. Improper budgetary practices reflect upon the individual and the program. The district has a right to expect that policy will be followed by all its employees.

The handling of cash should be kept at a minimum. However, there will be a good deal of cash flowing through a community school program. Fees from registration, cash for projects constructed in the shops and art programs, money from ticket sales, funds from special sales and community projects, dimes and nickels from vending machines will be part of the funds that are temporarily the responsibility of a community school director. This places the individual in a rather precarious position if there is inadequate protection of school funds through improper procedures. It is recommended that the following procedures be adopted.

1. Do bond all employees that have access to or responsibility for district money.

2. Do provide all instructors in classes that require payments (such as courses that require payments for project materials) with numbered receipt books and do insist on proper accounting.

3. Do provide collection every day or night as the case may be.

4. Do have someone other than the community school director collect money from vending machines. Also, do have someone other than the director responsible for the filling of the machines.

5. Do have a night deposit system. Never leave money in the building.

6. Do develop a system of ticket sales where beginning and ending numbers are kept and a strict accounting is maintained.

7. Do pay taxes on all tickets when applicable. An example could be:

<u>Ticket $1.25</u>
Admission $1.20
State Tax   <u> .05</u>
$1.25

8. Do pay all bills with checks.

9. Do use a postage meter.

10. Do carry the proper type and adequate insurance.

11. Do require a yearly audit of all accounts.

BIBLIOGRAPHY

BOOKS

Bereleson, Bernard and Steiner, Gary A. *Human Behavior, An Inventory of Scientific Findings.* New York: Harcourt, Brace and World, Inc., 1964.

Combs, Arthur W., (ed.,). *Perceiving, Behaving, Becoming.* Washington, D.C.: Yearbook, Association for Supervision and Curriculum Development, National Education Association, 1962.

Gibran, Kahlil. *The Prophet.* New York: Knoph, 1929.

Glasser, William. *Schools Without Failure.* New York: Harper and Row, 1969.

Hickey, Howard D. and Van Voorhees, Curtis and Associates. *The Role of the School in Community Education.* Midland, Michigan: Pendell Publishing Company, 1969.

Hunter, Floyd. *Community Power Structure.* Chapel Hill, N.C., 1953.

Kvaraceus, William C., (ed.). *Negro Self-Concept.* New York: McGraw-Hill, Inc., 1965.

Kelley, Earl C. *Education for What is Real.* New York: Harper and Row, Publishers Inc., 1947.

——————————— *In Defense of Youth.* Prentice-Hall Publishing Co., 1963.

Kerber, August and Smith, Wilfred, (ed.). *Educational Issues in a Changing Society.* Detroit: Wayne State University Press, 1964.

Morphet, Edgar O. and Ryan, Charles O. *Planning and Effecting Needed Change in Education.* Denver: (Eight State Project), 1967.

National Education Association and American Association of School Administrators, Educational Policies Commission. *National Policy and Financing of the Public Schools.* Washington, D.C.: 1959.

Passow, A. Harry, (ed.). *Education in Depressed Areas.* New York: Bureau of Publications, Teachers College, Columbia University, 1963.

Riessman, Frank. *The Culturally Deprived Child.* New York: Harper and Brothers Inc., 1962.

Sexton, Patricia Cayo. *Education and Income.* New York: Viking Press, Inc., 1961.

Stern, George. "Measuring Non-Cognitive Variables in Research on Teaching," *Handbook on Research on Teaching.* N.L. Gage, Editor. Chicago: Rand McNally Co., pp. 403-447.

ARTICLES AND PERIODICALS

Anderson, Joseph A. "The Economic Value of The Community School Concept to Business." *The Community School and Its Administration*, Vol. VII, No. 9 (May 1969), Ford Press, Inc., Midland, Michigan.

Bibliography

Bettelheim, Bruno. "Teaching the Disadvantaged." *NEA Journal*, Vol 54 (September, 1965), 8-11.

Cass, James. "The Crucial Years Before Six." *Saturday Review*, (June 15, 1968), p. 59.

_____ "Give Urban Schools Back to the People." *Saturday Review*, (December 17, 1968), p. 55.

Melby, Ernest O. "The Community School: A Social Imperative." *The Community School and Its Administration*, Vol. VII, No. 2 (October 1968), Ford Press, Inc., Midland, Michigan.

_____ "Decentralization and Community Control: Threat or Challenge?" *The Community School and Its Administration*, Vol. VIII, No. 3, (November 1969), Ford Press, Inc., Midland, Michigan.

Oliver, W.A. "Teachers Educational Beliefs Versus Their Classroom Practices." *Journal of Educational Research*, Vol. XLVII (September, 1953), pp. 48-49.

Phillips, Beeman N. "The Individual and the Classroom Group as Frames of Reference in Determining Teacher Effectiveness." *Journal of Educational Research*, Vol. 58 (November, 1964), 128-131.

Rich, John. "How Social Class Values Affect Teacher-Pupil Relations." *The Journal of Educational Sociology*, Vol. 33 (May, 1960), 355-359.

Roberts, Wallace. "The Battle for Urban Schools." *Saturday Review*, (Nov. 16, 1968), pp. 97-117.

Schultz, Theodore. "The Economic Value of Education." *The American Economic Review* Vol. 11, No. 1, (March, 1961).

Schwartz, Alfred. "A Search for Quality in Education." *The Great Plains Project School District Organization Project, Position Papers*. Lincoln: Nebraska, June, 1968, pp. 31-58.

Solberg, James. "Community Relations, I Want Them to Know That We Care." *School Management* (September, 1968), pp. 36-44.

Stebbins, Marion, "How to Use a Community School Director." *Nations Schools* (October, 1966).

UNPUBLISHED MATERIAL

Goldberg, Miriam. "Adapting Teacher Style of Pupil Differences." An Abstract, Report from Horace Mann-Lincoln Institute Report, New York (March, 1963)

Kerensky, V.M. "What Type of Education Can Make the Difference?" Unpublished Monograph, Florida Atlantic University, Boca Raton, Florida, September, 1968.

Kerensky, V.M. "Purposes of the Conference", N.C.S.E.A. Conference, Third National Community School Education Association Conference, Atlanta, Ga., December, 1968.

Lampshire, Richard, et. al. "Perry Community School Research Study." Unpublished Community Survey Questionnaire, Department of Educational Administration, Drake University, Spring, 1970.

Langerman, Arthur L. and Walker, James R. "Teacher Opinionaire." Unpublished Questionnaire, Department of Educational Administration, Drake University, Spring, 1970.

BROCHURES

THE FOLLOWING BROCHURES ARE AVAILABLE FROM THE FLINT BOARD OF EDUCA-
TION, FLINT, MICHIGAN.

"Community School Education"

"The Community School Director"

"The Police-School Liaison Program"

"The School Health and Safety Program"

"Vocational Guidance Program"

BIOGRAPHY

DR. ROBERT L. WHITT, PROFESSOR
COLLEGE OF EDUCATION
DRAKE UNIVERSITY
DES MOINES, IOWA 50311

Dr. Whitt is a native Californian. After serving in W.W. II, he returned to college at the College of the Pacific in Stockton, California.

Upon completion of college in January 1949, he became an elementary teacher in that community. From 1949 until 1954 he served as a teacher and vice-principal in ghetto schools, where he learned about community education first-hand.

In 1954, he became an elementary principal. In this new setting community education became imperative.

After three years as an elementary principal, he was moved to a jr. high school in Stockton, California where he was a director of curriculum and guidance. This experience enabled him to become a jr. high school principal in 1959.

In 1960 he took over as principal in a large senior high school in Stockton. This school was located in the slum area of the community and brought with it all the typical problems expected in such a setting.

In 1963, after three years as a successful high school principal, he was promoted to assistant superintendent of schools in charge of secondary education in Stockton, a district of some 33,000 pupils.

After serving one year in this role, he received a Mott Fellowship Grant to study in Flint, Michigan and at Wayne State University, Detroit. This program is designed to provide outstanding experiences in community education. He stayed in Flint two years, receiving his Ed. D. from Wayne State University in the spring of 1966.

Following the stay in Flint, he was given a position as Associate Professor of Educational Administration at Wayne State University where he continued to work with the Flint Internship Program.

In 1967 he was appointed chairman of the department of educational administration, Drake University, Des Moines, Iowa with the rank of full professor.

In 1970-71, Dr. Whitt will be working as an American Council of Education fellow as an administrative intern at the college level. He will be working with Dr. Paul Sharp, President of Drake University in preparation for an administrative position in university or college administration.

He has attended the University of California and Stanford University. He belongs to several academic honor societies and is now president of the Drake Chapter of Phi Kappa Phi.

He is married to Mrs. Jean Whitt and they have three children:
Elizabeth, 19 — A sophomore at Drake University.
Joanne,   17 — A freshman at Drake University.
Donald,   12 — A seventh grader in the Des Moines Community Schools.